P9-DCD-247

The
Fifth Gospel

The Fifth Gospel

The Gospel of Thomas Comes of Age

Stephen J. Patterson
and James M. Robinson

With a New English Translation
by Hans-Gebhard Bethge et al.

TRINITY PRESS INTERNATIONAL
Harrisburg, Pennsylvania

Copyright © 1998 by Stephen J. Patterson and James M. Robinson

All rights reserved. No part of this book may be reproduced, stored in a retrieval system, or transmitted, in any form or by any means, electronic, mechanical, photocopying, recording, or otherwise, without the written permission of the publisher.

Trinity Press International, P.O. Box 1321, Harrisburg, PA 17105
Trinity Press International is a division of the Morehouse Group

Library of Congress Cataloging-in-Publication Data

Patterson, Stephen J., 1957-
    The fifth Gospel : the Gospel of Thomas comes of age / Stephen J.
  Patterson and James M. Robinson.
        p.   cm.
    Includes bibliographical references and index.
    ISBN 1-56338-249-0 (pbk. : alk. paper)
    1. Gospel of Thomas – Criticism, interpretation, etc. 2. Nag
  Hammadi codices.   I. Robinson, James McConkey, 1924-   .
  II. Gospel of Thomas.   English.   III. Title.
  BS2860.T52P384   1998
  229'.8 – dc21   98-39836

Printed in the United States of America

00   01   02   03   04   10   9   8   7   6   5   4

For
Hans-Martin Schenke
in gratitude

Contents

Introduction

The Nag Hammadi library is a collection of ancient books discovered in Egypt in 1945, near the modern-day city of Nag Hammadi. An Egyptian peasant happened upon them where they lay, sealed in a rough clay jar buried in the talus at the base of the cliffs that line the Nile River in upper Egypt. These papyrus books (or codices), thirteen in all, date to the fourth century. They are written in Coptic, a new way to write the ancient tongue of Pharaonic Egypt still in use when Christians first came to Egypt in the late first or early second century. These early Christians used the Greek alphabet (together with a few characters unique to Coptic) to create a written form of this language, into which Christian works composed in Greek could be translated for use among the local population. The Nag Hammadi texts all share this history: they are Coptic translations of Greek originals made by Christian scribes for use in Egypt.

Within the thirteen volumes of the Nag Hammadi library were found almost fifty previously unknown or lost texts. Most of them are Christian tracts, though there are a number of Jewish and Hermetic texts, and at least one Greek philosophical text — a fragment of Plato's *Republic*. Thus, the Nag Hammadi library ranks among the major manuscript discoveries of the twentieth century of relevance to biblical studies. By far the most important of these newly discovered texts is the second tractate in Codex II of the library: the *Gospel of Thomas*.

The *Gospel of Thomas* is an ancient Christian gospel known from antiquity, but thought to have been lost — that is, until the Nag Hammadi discovery. It is not like the more

1

familiar gospels found in the New Testament, for it presents no story of Jesus, no accounts of his birth, life, death, or resurrection. Rather, it is a collection of 114 sayings ascribed to Jesus, each introduced with the simple formula, "Jesus says." A good number (about half) of these sayings were already known, since they are found also in the canonical gospels, principally in Matthew, Mark, and Luke. Of the remaining sayings, a few were known from an occasional reference or odd quote found scattered in the literature of early Christianity. But the vast majority were entirely unknown before this remarkable discovery.

The Coptic *Gospel of Thomas* from Nag Hammadi is our only complete version of this gospel. As with most of the Nag Hammadi texts, the Greek original is lost, save for a few fragments discovered as part of another famous papyrus find in Egypt, the Oxyrhynchus Papyri. Thus, when one speaks of the *Gospel of Thomas* today, it is usually to the Coptic version that one is referring. As with all ancient manuscripts, this single copy of *Thomas* has many errors and flaws — misspellings, omissions, holes in the papyrus — which scholars must try to correct and fill in before a proper translation can be made. In the case of New Testament texts, for which we have dozens of early manuscripts, this sort of critical work is facilitated by comparing different manuscripts with one another to arrive at the best original reading. In the case of *Thomas,* scholars must do this work without the advantage of comparison, since only one copy exists, and that a translation. It is much more difficult, painstaking, speculative, and sometimes simply impossible.

The first critical edition of the *Gospel of Thomas,* together with an English translation by the well-known British scholar R. McL. Wilson, appeared in 1959, just in time for the Christmas rush. It promptly sold over forty thousand copies! This very popular version of *Thomas* became the scholarly standard for many years to come. But it was produced before scholarship had advanced very far in understanding the textual problems in the manuscript and the many translational difficulties posed by the text. Since then scholars have continued to study *Thomas,* making advances that have made it possible to produce new and better texts and translations of this important document of early Christianity.

We are pleased to offer in the present volume a translation of *Thomas* that we believe represents the culmination of the best scholarship on *Thomas,* gathered over many years in the same center of research that produced the initial translation of *Thomas* — Berlin. Out of that early flurry of activity there emerged a team of scholars with the disarming self-designation: Berlin Working Group for Coptic Gnostic Writings (Berliner Arbeitskreis für koptisch-gnostische Schriften). Originally founded by Hans-Martin Schenke, it is led today by Schenke's former student Hans-Gebhard Bethge. The Berlin Working Group continues to be the most important center for the study of the Nag Hammadi texts. It is therefore not surprising that, as the fruit of more than a generation of concentrated work, they have produced a critical Coptic text of the *Gospel of Thomas* superior to any previously available. Furthermore, their translations into German and English provide the most reliable access to the sayings themselves. Their original Coptic text and translations are available in the latest editions of Kurt Aland's *Synopsis Quattuor Evangeliorum* (15th ed., 1996, 2d corrected printing, 1997), published by the German Bible Society.

The English translation presented here is an updated and editorially improved version of the 1996 Berlin Working Group's version, created by the coauthors of the present volume in consultation with Hans-Martin Schenke. In offering it to an English-speaking audience, we hope to make this text available to the novice and to the experienced scholar alike, as a way of encouraging further interest in this important text.

There are a number of standard sigla used in the translation to indicate various editorial decisions of the Berlin team:

( )   Parentheses surround a word or words not in the Coptic text itself, but which an English reader needs in order to catch the tone of the original.

< >   Pointed brackets surround a word or words where the translation involves a correction of an error in the manuscript.

[ ]   Square brackets indicate places where a hole in the manuscript had led to the loss of one or more words. Often the team is able to supply the missing word(s) by conjecture; other times the hole must be left blank.

{ }   Braces indicate that the translators have omitted something that occurs in the original manuscript on the assumption that it is in error.

In addition to this translation of *Thomas,* we have provided two essays for persons possibly unfamiliar with this new gospel or with the events that led to its discovery and publication. The first (by Patterson) is a general introduction to the *Gospel of Thomas* as it appears now fifty years after its discovery. The second (by Robinson) tells the story of that discovery, recounts the subsequent work of bringing the new gospel to light, and assesses how the Nag Hammadi discovery has changed the landscape of New Testament scholarship. These essays will initiate the general reader to the discussion of this new text and will indicate avenues for further investigation. For those interested in reading more about *Thomas* and the Nag Hammadi library, we have provided a brief annotated list, "For Further Reading."

More than fifty years have now passed since the discovery of the *Gospel of Thomas.* With this new text and these essays it is hoped that we will help to set the stage for another fifty years of scholarship and inquiry every bit as productive as the first fifty. In presenting them we wish to acknowledge especially the work of the Berlin Working Group for Coptic Gnostic Writings, whose current members include, in addition to Profs. Bethge and Schenke, Christina-Maria Franke, Judith Hartenstein, Uwe-Karsten Plisch, and Jens Schröter. Their collective expertise is what sets this publication apart and moves the translation of the *Gospel of Thomas* to a new level.

English Translation*

Introduction, Saying 1

These are the hidden words that the living Jesus spoke. And Didymos Judas Thomas wrote them down. And he said: "Whoever finds the meaning of these words will not taste death."

Saying 2

[1] Jesus says:[a] "The one who seeks should not cease seeking until he finds. [2] And when he finds, he will be dismayed. [3] And when he is dismayed, he will be astonished. [4] And he will be king over the All."

Saying 3

[1] Jesus says: "If those who lead you say to you: 'Look, the kingdom is in the sky!' then the birds of the sky will precede you.

[2] If they say to you: 'It is in the sea,' then the fishes will precede you.

[3] Rather, the kingdom is inside of you and outside of you."

[4] "When you come to know yourselves, then you will be known, and you will realize that you are the children of the

---

*Translation by the Berliner Arbeitskreis für koptisch-gnostische Schriften (Hans-Gebhard Bethge, Christina-Maria Franke, Judith Hartenstein, Uwe-Karsten Plisch, Hans-Martin Schenke, Jens Schröter), as modified by Stephen J. Patterson and James M. Robinson. It is taken from *Synopsis Quattuor Evangeliorum,* © 1996 Deutsche Bibelgesellschaft, Stuttgart, 2d corrected printing, 1997.

a. The verb can also be expressed in its past tense. When sayings appear without a narrative framework, a translation in the present tense is preferable.

7

living Father. [5]But if you do not come to know yourselves, then you exist in poverty and you are poverty."

Saying 4

[1]Jesus says: "The person old in his days will not hesitate to ask a child seven days old about the place of life, and he will live.
[2]For many who are first will become last,
[3]and they will become a single one."

Saying 5

[1]Jesus says: "Come to know what is in front of you, and that which is hidden from you will become clear to you. [2]For there is nothing hidden that will not become manifest."

Saying 6

[1]His disciples questioned him, (and) they said to him: "Do you want us to fast? And how should we pray and give alms? And what diet should we observe?"[a]

[2]Jesus says: "Do not lie. [3]And do not do what you hate.
[4]For everything is disclosed in view of <the truth>.[b]
[5]For there is nothing hidden that will not become revealed. [6]And there is nothing covered that will remain undisclosed."

Saying 7

[1]Jesus says: "Blessed is the lion that a person will eat and the lion will become human. [2]And anathema is the person whom a lion will eat and the lion will become human."[c]

---

a. Cf. Saying 14:1–3.

b. The Coptic text reads "before the face of heaven," though this is probably a mistake. The emendation is proposed on the basis of Oxyrhynchus Papyrus 654.38.

c. The phrase "and the lion will become human" could be a copyist's error that may have even occurred already in the underlying Greek *Vorlage,* and can possibly be deleted. Although emendation to "and the person will be the lion" produces a formal parallelism, it is not unproblematic with regard to content.

Saying 8

[1] And he says: "The human being is like a sensible fisherman who cast his net into the sea and drew it up from the sea filled with little fish. [2] Among them the sensible fisherman found a large, fine fish. [3] He threw all the little fish back into the sea, (and) he chose the large fish effortlessly.

[4] Whoever has ears to hear should hear."

Saying 9

[1] Jesus says: "Look, a sower went out. He filled his hands (with seeds), (and) he scattered (them). [2] Some fell on the path, and the birds came and pecked them up. [3] Others fell on the rock, and did not take root in the soil, and they did not put forth ears. [4] And others fell among the thorns, they choked the seeds, and worms ate them. [5] And others fell on good soil, and it produced good fruit. It yielded sixty per measure and one hundred and twenty per measure."

Saying 10

Jesus says: "I have cast fire upon the world, and see, I am guarding it until it blazes."[a]

Saying 11

[1] Jesus says: "This heaven will pass away, and the (heaven) above it will pass away.

[2] And the dead are not alive, and the living will not die.

[3] In the days when you consumed what was dead, you made it alive. When you are in the light, what will you do?

[4] On the day when you were one, you became two. But when you become two, what will you do?"

Saying 12

[1] The disciples said to Jesus: "We know that you will depart from us. Who (then) will rule[b] over us?"

---

a. Or: "I am protecting it (the world) until it blazes."

b. Literally: "be great."

²Jesus said to them: "No matter where you came from, you should go to James the Just, for whose sake heaven and earth came into being."

Saying 13

¹Jesus said to his disciples: "Compare me and tell me whom I am like."

²Simon Peter said to him: "You are like a just messenger."*ᵃ*

³Matthew said to him: "You are like an (especially) wise philosopher."

⁴Thomas said to him: "Teacher, my mouth cannot bear at all to say whom you are like."

⁵Jesus said: "I am not your teacher. For you have drunk, you have become intoxicated at the bubbling spring that I have measured out."

⁶And he took him, (and) withdrew, (and) he said three words to him.

⁷But when Thomas came back to his companions, they asked him: "What did Jesus say to you?"

⁸Thomas said to them: "If I tell you one of the words he said to me, you will pick up stones and throw them at me, and fire will come out of the stones (and) burn you up."

Saying 14

¹Jesus said to them: "If you fast, you will bring forth sin for yourselves. ²And if you pray, you will be condemned. ³And if you give alms, you will do harm to your spirits."*ᵇ*

⁴"And if you go into any land and wander from place to place,*ᶜ* (and) if they take you in, (then) eat what they will set before you. Heal the sick among them!*ᵈ*

⁵For what goes into your mouth will not defile you. Rather, what comes out of your mouth will defile you."

---

a. Cf. Luke 7:24; 9:52. Other translations use "angel" for *angelos*, rather than "messenger."

b. Cf. Saying 6:1.

c. Literally: "in the countryside."

d. Or: "there (in the countryside)."

Saying 15

Jesus says: "When you see one who was not born of woman, fall on your face (and) worship him. That one is your Father."

Saying 16

[1] Jesus says: "Perhaps people think that I have come to cast peace upon the earth. [2] But they do not know that I have come to cast dissension upon the earth: fire, sword, war.

[3] For there will be five in one house: there will be three against two and two against three, father against son and son against father.

[4] And they will stand as solitary ones."

Saying 17

Jesus says: "I will give you what no eye has seen, and what no ear has heard, and what no hand has touched, and what has not occurred to the human mind."[a]

Saying 18

[1] The disciples said to Jesus: "Tell us how our end will be."

[2] Jesus said: "Have you already discovered the beginning that you are now asking about the end? For where the beginning is, there the end will be too.

[3] Blessed is he who will stand at the beginning. And he will know the end, and he will not taste death."

Saying 19

[1] Jesus says: "Blessed is he who was, before he came into being.

[2] If you become disciples of mine (and) listen to my words, these stones will serve you.

[3] For you have five trees in Paradise that do not change during summer (and) winter, and their leaves do not fall. [4] Whoever comes to know them will not taste death."

---

a. Cf. 1 Cor. 2:9; *Dialogue of the Savior* (Nag Hammadi Codex III,5) p. 140, 2f.

Saying 20

[1] The disciples said to Jesus: "Tell us whom the kingdom of heaven is like!"

[2] He said to them: "It is like a mustard seed. [3] <It>[a] is the smallest of all seeds. [4] But when it falls on cultivated soil, it produces a large branch (and) becomes shelter for the birds of the sky."

Saying 21

[1] Mary said to Jesus: "Whom are your disciples like?"

[2] He said: "They are like servants[b] who are entrusted with a field that is not theirs. [3] When the owners of the field arrive, they will say: 'Let us have our field.' [4] (But) they are naked[c] in their presence so as to let them have it, (and thus) to give them their field."

[5] "That is why I say: When the master of the house learns that the thief is about to come, he will be on guard before he comes (and) will not let him break into his house, his domain,[d] to carry away his possessions.

[6] (But) you, be on guard against the world! [7] Gird your loins with great strength, so that the robbers will not find a way to get to you."

[8] "For the necessities for which you wait (with longing) will be found.[e]

[9] There ought to be a wise person among you! [10] When the

---

a. The conjugational element is missing in the Coptic text due to haplography.

b. The usual (literal) translation of *šēre šēm* as "little children" makes little sense in this passage; the translation given here takes *šēre šēm* to be a rendering of *pais* (meaning *doulos*, cf. Matt. 14:2 and 2 Kings 11:24 LXX) in the Coptic translator's Greek copy.

c. Probably there is an ellipsis in the Coptic text. It is also possible that something has been left out in the transmission of the text.

d. The Coptic genitive here is to be understood as an explicative genitive.

e. Alternative translation (cf. Saying 21:6f.): "For the possessions you are guarding they will find."

fruit was ripe, he came quickly with his sickle in hand, (and) he harvested it.

¹¹Whoever has ears to hear should hear."

Saying 22

¹Jesus saw infants being suckled.*

²He said to his disciples: "These little ones being suckled are like those who enter the kingdom."

³They said to him: "Then will we enter the kingdom as little ones?"

⁴Jesus said to them: "When you make the two into one and when you make the inside like the outside and the outside like the inside and the above like the below — ⁵that is, to make the male and the female into a single one, so that the male will not be male and the female will not be female* — ⁶and when you make eyes instead of an eye and a hand instead of a hand and a foot instead of a foot, an image instead of an image,* ⁷then you will enter [the kingdom]."

Saying 23

¹Jesus says: "I will choose you, one from a thousand and two from ten thousand. ²And they will stand as a single one."

Saying 24

¹His disciples said: "Show us the place where you are, because it is necessary for us to seek it."

²He said to them: "Whoever has ears should hear!

³Light exists inside a person of light, and he* shines on the whole world. If he does not shine, there is darkness."

---

a. Literally: "receiving milk."

b. It is possible that something has been omitted at the beginning of Saying 22:5, so that the original text would have read: "and <I have come> to make...."

c. It is possible also for the Coptic here to mean "face"; cf. *Acts of Peter and the Twelve Apostles* (Nag Hammadi Codex VI,1) p. 2, 24.

d. Also possible is the translation: "it shines... If it does not shine...."

Saying 25

[1]Jesus says: "Love your brother like your life! [2]Protect him like the apple of your eye!"

Saying 26

[1]Jesus says: "You see the splinter that is in your brother's eye, but you do not see the beam that is in your (own) eye. [2]When you remove the beam from your (own) eye, then you will see clearly (enough) to remove the splinter from your brother's eye."

Saying 27

[1]"If you do not abstain from the world,*a* you will not find the kingdom.

[2]If you do not make the Sabbath into a Sabbath,*b* you will not see the Father."

Saying 28

[1]Jesus says: "I stood in the middle of the world, and in flesh I appeared to them. [2]I found all of them drunk. None of them did I find thirsty. [3]And my soul ached for the children of humanity, because they are blind in their heart, and they cannot see; for they came into the world empty, (and) they also seek to depart from the world empty. [4]But now they are drunk. (But) when they shake off their wine, then they will change their mind."

Saying 29

[1]Jesus says: "If the flesh came into being because of the spirit, it is a wonder. [2]But if the spirit (came into being) because of the body, it is a wonder of wonders."

[3]Yet I marvel at how this great wealth has taken up residence in this poverty.

---

a. Literally: "If you do not fast against the world."
b. Or: "keep the Sabbath as a Sabbath."

Saying 30

[1] Jesus says: "Where there are three gods, they are gods.[a]
[2] Where there are two or one, I am with him."

Saying 31

[1] Jesus says: "No prophet is accepted in his (own) village.
[2] A physician does not heal those who know him."

Saying 32

Jesus says: "A city built upon a high mountain (and) fortified cannot fall, nor can it be hidden."

Saying 33

[1] Jesus says: "What you will hear with your ear {with the other ear}[b] proclaim from your rooftops.
[2] For no one lights a lamp (and) puts it under a bushel, nor does he put it in a hidden place. [3] Rather, he puts it on a lampstand, so that everyone who comes in and goes out will see its light."

Saying 34

Jesus says: "If a blind (person) leads a blind (person), both will fall into a pit."

Saying 35

[1] Jesus says: "It is not possible for someone to enter the house of a strong (person) (and) take it by force unless he binds his hands. [2] Then he will loot his house."

---

a. The Coptic text is probably corrupt. On the basis of Oxyrhynchus Papyrus 1.23 it should be read: "Where there are three, they are godless."

b. The text is probably corrupt, due to dittography; nevertheless, there exist two possibilities for understanding the transmitted text as sensible. Either: "...with your ear, proclaim from your rooftops into someone else's ear"; or: "...with your (one) ear (and) with (your) other ear proclaim" (as an idiomatic wordplay paraphrasing "with both ears").

Saying 36

Jesus says: "Do not worry from morning to evening and from evening to morning about what you will wear."[a]

Saying 37

[1]His disciples said: "When will you appear to us, and when will we see you?"

[2]Jesus said: "When you undress without being ashamed[b] and take your clothes (and) put them under your feet like little children (and) trample on them, [3]then [you] will see the son of the Living One, and you will not be afraid."

Saying 38

[1]Jesus says: "Many times you have desired to hear these words, these that I am speaking to you, and you have no one else from whom to hear them.

[2]There will be days when you will seek me, (and) you will not find me."[c]

Saying 39

[1]Jesus says: "The Pharisees and the scribes have received the keys of knowledge, (but) they have hidden them.[d] [2]Neither have they entered, nor have they allowed to enter those who wished to.

[3]You, however, be as shrewd as serpents and as innocent as doves!"

---

a. Oxyrhynchus Papyrus 655.1.1–17 has a much longer text of Saying 36: "[1][Jesus says, Do not be anxious] from morning [to late nor] from evening [to] morning, neither [about] your [food], what [you will] eat, [nor] about [your clothing], what you [will] wear. [2][You are far] better than the [lilies] which [do not] card nor [spin]. [3]Not having any garment, what [will you put on], you too? [4]Who might add to your stature? He will give you your garment."

b. Or: "When you take off your shame."

c. Cf. Sayings 92; 59.

d. Or: "took away the keys of knowledge and have hidden them."

Saying 40

¹Jesus says: "A grapevine was planted outside (the vineyard) of the Father. ²And since it is not supported, it will be pulled up by its root (and) will perish."

Saying 41

¹Jesus says: "Whoever has (something) in his hand, (something more) will be given to him.

²And whoever has nothing, even the little he has will be taken from him."

Saying 42

Jesus says: "Become passers-by."

Saying 43

¹His disciples said to him: "Who are you to say this to us?"

²"Do you not realize from what I say to you who I am?

³But you have become like the Jews! They love the tree, (but) they hate its fruit. Or they love the fruit, (but) they hate the tree."

Saying 44

¹Jesus says: "Whoever blasphemes against the Father, it will be forgiven him. ²And whoever blasphemes against the Son, it will be forgiven him. ³But whoever blasphemes against the Holy Spirit, it will not be forgiven him, neither on earth nor in heaven."

Saying 45

¹Jesus says: "Grapes are not harvested from thorns, nor are figs picked from thistles, for they do not produce fruit.

²A good person brings forth good from his treasure. ³A bad person brings (forth) evil from the bad*a* treasure that is in his heart, and (in fact) he speaks evil. ⁴For out of the abundance of the heart he brings forth evil."

---

a. Literally: "his bad."

Saying 46

¹Jesus says: "From Adam to John the Baptist, among those born of women there is no one who surpasses John the Baptist so that his (i.e., John's) eyes need not be downcast."*a*

² "But I have (also) said: 'Whoever among you becomes little will know the kingdom and will surpass John.' "

Saying 47

¹Jesus says: "It is impossible for a person to mount two horses and to stretch two bows.

²And it is impossible for a servant to serve two masters. Else he will honor the one and insult the other."

³ "No person drinks old wine and immediately desires to drink new wine.

⁴And new wine is not put into old wineskins, so that they do not burst; nor is old wine put into (a) new wineskin, so that it does not spoil it.

⁵An old patch is not sewn onto a new garment, because a tear will result."

Saying 48

Jesus says: "If two make peace with one another in one and the same house, (then) they will say to the mountain: 'Move away,' and it will move away."

Saying 49

¹Jesus says: "Blessed are the solitary ones,*b* the elect. For you will find the kingdom. ²For you come from it (and) will return to it."

---

a. It is possible that the text is corrupt. Instead of the consecutive understanding of *šina*, a final (but hardly a causal) understanding is also possible. Consequently the literal translation would be: "so that his eyes do not get broken" or "so that his eyes do not fail."

b. *auō* is to be understood as an equivalent to an epexegetical *kai* and not as a copula.

Saying 50

[1] Jesus says: "If they say to you: 'Where do you come from?' (then) say to them: 'We have come from the light, the place where the light has come into being by itself, has established [itself] and has appeared in their image.'

[2] If they say to you: 'Is it you?'[a] (then) say: 'We are his children, and we are the elect of the living Father.'

[3] If they ask you: 'What is the sign of your Father among you?' (then) say to them: 'It is movement and repose.' "

Saying 51

[1] His disciples said to him: "When will the <resurrection>[b] of the dead take place, and when will the new world come?"

[2] He said to them: "That (resurrection) which you are awaiting has (already) come, but you do not recognize it."

Saying 52

[1] His disciples said to him: "Twenty-four prophets have spoken in Israel, and all (of them) have spoken through you."[c]

[2] He said to them: "You have pushed away the living (one) from yourselves, and you have begun[d] to speak of those who are dead."

Saying 53

[1] His disciples said to him: "Is circumcision beneficial, or not?"

[2] He said to them: "If it were beneficial, their father would beget them circumcised from their mother. [3] But the true circumcision in the spirit has prevailed over everything."[e]

---

a. One could possibly emend to: "<Who> are you?"

b. The Coptic reads "repose," but this seems to be a misunderstanding caused by the end of Saying 50:3. Cf. 2 Tim. 2:18.

c. Possible alternative translations are: "in you" or "of you" or "about you." It depends on which Greek preposition is expressed by the Coptic version.

d. Behind the Coptic expression seems to be a Greek ingressive aorist.

e. Literally: "has found absolute profit (or use)."

Saying 54

Jesus says: "Blessed are the poor. For the kingdom of heaven belongs to you."

Saying 55

[1] Jesus says: "Whoever does not hate his father and his mother cannot become a disciple of mine.

[2] And whoever does not hate his brothers and his sisters (and) will not take up his cross as I do, will not be worthy of me."

Saying 56

[1] Jesus says: "Whoever has come to know the world has found a corpse. [2] And whoever has found (this) corpse, of him the world is not worthy."

Saying 57

[1] Jesus says: "The kingdom of the Father is like a person who had (good) seed. [2] His enemy came by night. He sowed darnel among the good seed. [3] The person did not allow (the servants) to pull up the darnel. He said to them: 'Lest you go to pull up the darnel (and then) pull up the wheat along with it.'[a]

[4] For on the day of the harvest the darnel will be apparent[b] and it will be pulled up (and) burned."

---

a. The translation of the *mēpōs* clause explaining the reason for the apprehension presupposes a conjecture: that *je enahōle* is to be seen as a corruption of an original *je etetnahōle*. But it is also possible that there is an ellipsis in the Coptic text, such that the following should be understood: "Lest you go (saying): 'We will pull up the darnel,' (and then) pull up the wheat along with them." It is also possible that the Coptic text is to be explained by assuming that a whole line has been omitted through homoioteleuton, for instance: "Lest you go <and say: 'We want to go> in order to pull up the darnel.'..."

b. Or: "visible."

Saying 58

Jesus says: "Blessed is the person who has struggled.[a] He has found life."

Saying 59

Jesus says: "Look for the Living One while you are alive, so that you will not die and (then) seek to see him. And you will not be able to see (him)."[b]

Saying 60

[1] <He saw> a Samaritan who was trying to steal a lamb[c] while he was on his way to Judea.

[2] He said to his disciples: "That (person) is stalking the lamb."[d]

[3] They said to him: "So that he may kill it (and) eat it."

[4] He said to them: "As long as it is alive he will not eat it, but (only) when he has killed it (and) it has become a corpse."

[5] They said: "Otherwise he cannot do it."

[6] He said to them: "You, too, look for a place for your repose so that you may not become a corpse (and) get eaten."

Saying 61

[1] Jesus said: "Two will rest on a bed. The one will die, the other will live."

[2] Salome said: "(So) who are you, man? You have gotten a place on my couch as a <stranger>[e] and you have eaten from my table."

---

a. Or: "suffered."

b. Cf. Saying 38.

c. The Coptic text is to be understood in the sense of an expression *de conatu*.

d. Literally: "That (person) is around the lamb." Presumably *mpkōte n* corresponds to *einai peri ti* ("to be occupied with something"). The translation presupposes this understanding of the text.

e. Originally the Greek *Vorlage* might have had *hōs xenos* (= *hōs šmmo*) which was transmitted by an erroneous reading or understanding as *hōs ex henos* (= *hōs ebol hn oua*).

³Jesus said to her: "I am he who comes from the one who is (always) the same. I was given some of that which is my Father's."

⁴"I am your disciple!"

⁵Therefore I say: If someone becomes < like >ᵃ (God), he will become full of light. But if he becomes one, separated (from God), he will become full of darkness.

Saying 62

¹Jesus says: "I tell my mysteries to those who [are worthy] of [my] mysteries."

²"Whatever your right hand does, your left hand should not know what it is doing."

Saying 63

¹Jesus says: "There was a rich person who had many possessions. ²He said: 'I will use my possessions so that I might sow, reap, plant, (and) fill my storehouses with fruit so that I will not lack anything.' ³This was what he was thinking in his heart. And in that night he died.

⁴Whoever has ears should hear."

Saying 64

¹Jesus says: "A person had guests. And when he had prepared the dinner, he sent his servant so that he might invite the guests. ²He came to the first (and) said to him: 'My master invites you.' ³He said: 'I have bills for some merchants. They are coming to me this evening. I will go (and) give instructions to them. Excuse me from the dinner.'

⁴He came to another (and) said to him: 'My master has invited you.' ⁵He said to him: 'I have bought a house, and I have been called (away) for a day. I will not have time.' ⁶He went to another (and) said to him: 'My master invites

---

a. The manuscript reads, "If someone is destroyed, ... "

you.' [7]He said to him: 'My friend is going to marry, and I am the one who is going to prepare the meal. I will not be able to come. Excuse me from the dinner.' [8]He came to another (and) said to him: 'My master invites you.' [9]He said to him: 'I have bought a village. Since I am going to collect the rent, I will not be able to come. Excuse me.' [10]The servant went away. He said to his master: 'Those whom you invited to dinner have asked to be excused.' [11]The master said to his servant: 'Go out on the roads. Bring (back) whomever you find, so that they might have dinner.'

[12]Dealers and merchants [will] not enter the places of my Father."

Saying 65

[1]He said: "A [usurer][a] owned a vineyard. He gave it to some farmers so that they would work it (and) he might receive its fruit from them. [2]He sent his servant so that the farmers might give him the fruit of the vineyard. [3]They seized his servant, beat him, (and) almost killed him. The servant went (back and) told his master. [4]His master said: 'Perhaps <they> did not recognize <him>.'[b] [5]He sent another servant, (and) the farmers beat that other one as well. [6]Then the master sent his son (and) said: 'Perhaps they will show respect for my son.' [7](But) those farmers, since they knew that he was[c] the heir of the vineyard, seized him (and) killed him.

[8]Whoever has ears should hear."

Saying 66

Jesus says: "Show me the stone that the builders have rejected. It is the cornerstone."

---

a. The lacuna in the manuscript also allows the restoration of "[gracious (or: good)] person."

b. The manuscript reads, "Perhaps he did not recognize them"; the text is presumably corrupt.

c. Literally: "know that he is."

Saying 67

Jesus says: "Whoever knows all, if he is lacking one thing, he is (already) lacking everything."[a]

Saying 68

[1] Jesus says: "Blessed are you when(ever) they hate you (and) persecute you.

[2] But they (themselves) will find no place there where they have persecuted you."

Saying 69

[1] Jesus says: "Blessed are those who have been persecuted in their heart.[b] They are the ones who have truly come to know the Father."

[2] "Blessed are those who suffer from hunger so that the belly of the one who wishes (it) will be satisfied."

Saying 70

[1] Jesus says: "If you bring it into being within you, (then) that which you have will save you. [2] If you do not have it within you, (then) that which you do not have within you [will] kill you."

Saying 71

Jesus says: "I will [destroy this] house, and no one will be able to build it [again]."

Saying 72

[1] A [person said] to him: "Tell my brothers that they have to divide my father's possessions with me."

[2] He said to him: "Man, who made me a divider?"

[3] He turned to his disciples (and) said to them: "I am not a divider, am I?"

---

a. One should possibly emend to: "Whoever knows all but is lacking in himself, \<he\> is utterly lacking."

b. Perhaps the text is corrupt and originally read, analogously to Matt. 5:8, "Blessed are the persecuted, \<insofar as they are pure\> in their hearts."

Saying 73

Jesus says: "The harvest is plentiful but there are few workers. But beg the Lord that he may send workers into the harvest."

Saying 74

He said: "Lord, there are many around the well, but there is nothing*a* in the <well>."*b*

Saying 75

Jesus says: "Many are standing before the door, but it is the solitary ones who will enter the wedding hall."*c*

Saying 76

[1] Jesus says: "The kingdom of the Father is like a merchant who had merchandise and found a pearl. [2] That merchant is prudent. He sold the goods (and) bought for himself the pearl alone.

[3] You too look for his treasure, which does not perish, (and) which stays where no moth can reach it to eat it, and no worm destroys it."

Saying 77

[1] Jesus says: "I am the light that is over all. I am the All. The All came forth out of me. And to me the All has come."

[2] "Split a piece of wood — I am there.
[3] Lift the stone, and you will find me there."

Saying 78

[1] Jesus says: "Why did you go out to the countryside? To see a reed shaken by the wind, [2] and to see a person dressed in soft clothing [like your] kings and your great persons?*d*

a. Or: "nobody."
b. The manuscript reads (erroneously) "illness."
c. Cf. Matt. 25:1–13.
d. Or: "powerful persons."

³They are dressed in soft clothing and will not be able to recognize the truth."

Saying 79

¹A woman in the crowd said to him: "Hail to the womb that carried you and to the breasts that fed you."

²He said to [her]: "Hail to those who have heard the word of the Father (and) have truly kept it.

³For there will be days when you will say: 'Hail to the womb that has not conceived and to the breasts that have not given milk.'"

Saying 80

¹Jesus says: "Whoever has come to know the world has found the (dead) body. ²But whoever has found the (dead) body, of him the world is not worthy."

Saying 81

¹Jesus says: "Whoever has become rich should be king.
²And the one who has power should renounce*ᵃ* (it)."

Saying 82

¹Jesus says: "The person who is near me is near the fire.
²And the person who is far from me is far from the kingdom."

Saying 83

¹Jesus says: "The images are visible to humanity, but the light within them is hidden in the image.

²{}*ᵇ* The light of the Father will reveal itself, but his image is hidden by his light."

Saying 84

¹Jesus says: "When you see your likeness you are full of joy. ²But when you see your likenesses that came into exis-

---

a. Or: "reject," "refuse," "deny."
b. The manuscript reads "of."

tence before you — they neither die nor become manifest —
how much will you bear?"

Saying 85

¹Jesus says: "Adam came from a great power and great
wealth. But he did not become worthy of you. ²For if he had
been worthy, (then) [he would] not [have tasted] death."

Saying 86

¹Jesus says: "[Foxes have] their holes and birds have their
nest. ²But the son of man has no place to lay his head down
(and) to rest."

Saying 87

¹Jesus said: "Wretched is the body that depends on a body.
²And wretched is the soul that depends on these two."

Saying 88

¹Jesus says: "The messengers*a* and the prophets are coming to you, and they will give you what belongs to you. ²And
you, in turn, give to them what you have in your hands (and)
say to yourselves: 'When will they come (and) take what
belongs to them?' "

Saying 89

¹Jesus says: "Why do you wash the outside of the cup?
²Do you not understand that the one who created the inside
is also the one who created the outside?"

Saying 90

¹Jesus says: "Come to me, for my yoke is gentle*b* and my
lordship is mild. ²And you will find repose for yourselves."

---

a. Other translations prefer "angels" to "messengers" here. Cf. note to
Saying 13:2.
b. Or: "easy."

Saying 91

¹They said to him: "Tell us who you are so that we may believe in you."

²He said to them: "You examine the face of sky and earth, but the one who is before you, you have not recognized, and you do not know how to test this opportunity."[a]

Saying 92

¹Jesus says: "Seek and you will find.

²But the things you asked me about in past times, and what I did not tell you in that day, now I am willing to tell you, but you do not seek them."[b]

Saying 93

¹"Do not give what is holy to the dogs, lest they throw it upon the dunghill.

²Do not throw pearls to swine, lest they turn <them>[c] into [mud]."[d]

Saying 94

¹Jesus [says]: "The one who seeks will find.

²[The one who knocks], to that one will it be opened."

Saying 95

¹[Jesus says:] "If you have money, do not lend (it) out at interest. ²Rather, give [it] to the one from whom you will not get it (back)."[e]

Saying 96

¹Jesus [says]: "The kingdom of the Father is like [a] woman. ²She took a little bit of yeast. [She] hid it in dough (and) made it into huge loaves of bread.

---

a. Or: "right moment."

b. Cf. Saying 38.

c. The manuscript erroneously uses the singular.

d. Alternative restorations are possible, for instance: "lest they [destroy] <them>" or "lest they break <them> [into pieces]."

e. Or: "to the one from whom you will not get it (the interest)."

³Whoever has ears should hear."

Saying 97

¹Jesus says: "The kingdom of the [Father] is like a woman who is carrying a [jar] filled with flour. ²While she was walking on [the] way, very distant (from home), the handle of the jar broke (and) the flour leaked out [on] the path. ³(But) she did not know (it); she had not noticed a problem. ⁴When she reached her house, she put the jar down on the floor (and) found it empty."

Saying 98

¹Jesus says: "The kingdom of the Father is like a person who wanted to kill a powerful*ᵃ* person. ²He drew the sword in his house (and) stabbed it into the wall to test whether his hand would be strong (enough). ³Then he killed the powerful one."

Saying 99

¹The disciples said to him: "Your brothers and your mother are standing outside."

²He said to them: "Those here, who do the will of my Father, they are my brothers and my mother. ³They are the ones who will enter the kingdom of my Father."

Saying 100

¹They showed Jesus a gold coin and said to him: "Caesar's people demand taxes from us."

²He said to them: "Give Caesar (the things) that are Caesar's. ³Give God (the things) that are God's. ⁴And what is mine give me."

Saying 101

¹"Whoever does not hate his [father] and his mother as I do will not be able to be a [disciple] of mine. ²And whoever

---

a. Or: "noble."

does [not] love his [father and] his mother as I do will not be able to be a [disciple] of mine.

³For my mother [...],ᵃ but my true [mother] gave me life."

Saying 102

Jesus says: "Woe to them, the Pharisees, for they are like a dog sleepingᵇ in a cattle trough, for it neither eats nor [lets] the cattle eat."

Saying 103

Jesus says: "Blessed is the person who knows at which point (of the house)ᶜ the robbers are going to enter, so that [he] may arise to gather together his [domain] and gird his loins before they enter."

Saying 104

¹They said to [Jesus]: "Come, let us pray and fast today!"

²Jesus said: "What sin is it that I have committed, or wherein have I been overcome? ³But when the bridegroom comes out of the wedding chamber, then let (us) fast and pray."

Saying 105

Jesus says: "Whoever will come to know father and mother, he will be called son of a whore."ᵈ

---

a. The lacuna can be filled as follows: "For my mother, who has [given birth to me, has destroyed me]." Another possibility: "For my mother has [deceived me]."

b. Or: "lying."

c. Or: "at what part (of the night)."

d. Cf. *Gospel of Philip* (Nag Hammadi Codex II,3, p. 52, 21–24). As the text has been transmitted, an original negation may have been left out, so that we can understand the text as follows: "Whoever will not know father and mother...."

Saying 106

[1] Jesus says: "When you make the two into one, you will become sons of man.[a]

[2] And when you say: 'Mountain, move away,' it will move away."

Saying 107

[1] Jesus says: "The kingdom is like a shepherd who had a hundred sheep. [2] One of them went astray, the largest. He left the ninety-nine, (and) he sought the one until he found it. [3] After he had toiled, he said to the sheep: 'I love you more than the ninety-nine.' "

Saying 108

[1] Jesus says: "Whoever will drink from my mouth will become like me. [2] I myself will become he [3] and what is hidden will be revealed to him."

Saying 109

[1] Jesus says: "The kingdom is like a person who has a hidden treasure in his field, [of which] he knows nothing. [2] And [after] he had died, he left it to his [son]. (But) the son did not know (about it either). He took over that field (and) sold [it]. [3] And the one who had bought it came, and while he was ploughing [he found] the treasure. He began to lend money at interest to whom he wished."

Saying 110

Jesus says: "The one who has found the world (and) has become wealthy[b] should renounce[c] the world."

Saying 111

[1] Jesus says: "The heavens will roll up before you, and the earth.

---

a. Or: "children of humanity."

b. Possibly: "The one who <will> find the world (and) become wealthy."

c. Or: "deny," "reject," "refuse."

²And whoever is living from the living one will not see death."

³Does not*ᵃ* Jesus say: "Whoever has found himself, of him the world is not worthy"?

Saying 112

¹Jesus says: "Woe to the flesh that depends on the soul. ²Woe to the soul that depends on the flesh."

Saying 113

¹His disciples said to him: "The kingdom — on what day will it come?"

²"It will not come by watching (and waiting for) it. ³They will not say: 'Look, here!' or 'Look, there!' ⁴Rather, the kingdom of the Father is spread out upon the earth, and people do not see it."

Saying 114

¹Simon Peter said to them: "Let Mary go away from us, for women are not worthy of life."

²Jesus said: "Look, I will draw her in so as to make her male, so that she too may become a living male*ᵇ* spirit, similar to you."

³(But I say to you)*ᶜ*: "Every woman who makes herself male will enter the kingdom of heaven."

Subscription
The Gospel according to Thomas

---

a. We find here an ellipsis; perhaps we can assume the following Greek text: (*ē*) *ouk* (*oidate*) *hoti,* "(or do you) not (know) that...."

b. With regard to *n̲hoout,* we understand the *n* as functioning in an attributive sense belonging to *oupn̅a.* It should not be understood as a particle of identity.

c. Most of the translations and editions understand the *je* in a causal sense. But we are convinced that here we have the introduction of direct speech without an antecedent, presented in an elliptic form. Here we conjecture a *tijō de m̲mos nētn̲* ("but I say to you").

Understanding the Gospel of Thomas Today

STEPHEN J. PATTERSON

1. The Discovery of a New Gospel

Discoveries in the world of biblical studies are always exciting. The books of the Bible are ancient texts, shrouded in the mysteries of the remote past, a time and place about which we know precious little. We long for more information, any tidbit of evidence that might open up one more shadowy corner of the ancient world to our eager eyes. New discoveries excite us because they hold out the promise and possibility for disclosure. But rarely do the greatly heralded discoveries of the past live up to our inflated expectations of them. The discovery of the Dead Sea Scrolls is an exceptional case, as are a handful of less well-known discoveries, such as the Chester Beatty and the Bodmer papyri.

The discovery of the Nag Hammadi library falls into this rare category of astounding finds. It is probably the most important discovery of the twentieth century for the study of the New Testament and Christian origins, and yet it went completely unnoticed in 1945. That was the year in which an Egyptian peasant happened upon this remarkable cache of texts sealed in an ancient clay jar buried for safekeeping at the base of the cliffs that run along the Nile in upper Egypt, near the present-day town of Nag Hammadi.[1] But in

---

1. The complete story of this discovery was not told until James M.

the years since that fateful day, it has become clear that this is one discovery that has lived up to its promise. Among the many reasons that allow one to make this claim, none is as significant as the second tractate in codex two of the Nag Hammadi library, the text known today as the *Gospel of Thomas.*

The *Gospel of Thomas* was not always known by this name. Half a century before the famous discovery at Nag Hammadi, two British explorers, B. P. Grenfell and A. S. Hunt, had actually found fragments of this lost gospel among the ancient papyrus rubbish heaps of Oxyrhynchus, some two hundred kilometers downstream from Nag Hammadi. But these fragments held only a few sayings of the *Gospel of Thomas,* and no title or any indication of where the sayings might have come from. Grenfell and Hunt called them simply "Sayings of Our Lord," "New Sayings of Jesus," and a "Fragment of a Lost Gospel."[2] With the discovery of the new text from Nag Hammadi, it soon became clear that what Grenfell and Hunt had discovered were fragments of the lost *Gospel of Thomas.*[3]

Robinson investigated the circumstances in the 1970s and published his account in "The Discovery of the Nag Hammadi Codices" (*Biblical Archaeologist* 42, no. 4 [1979]: 206–24, and "Getting the Nag Hammadi Library into English," *Biblical Archaeologist* 42, no. 4 [1979]: 239–48). Robinson's essay in the present volume offers an updated version of this story.

2. These fragmentary Oxyrhynchus papyri, identified today as parts of the *Gospel of Thomas,* are known by their publication numbers POxy 1, POxy 654, and POxy 655. Grenfell and Hunt originally published POxy 1 in a pamphlet entitled *Logia Iesou: Sayings of Our Lord* (London: Henry Frowde, 1897). They published POxy 654 and 655 as *New Sayings of Jesus and Fragment of a Lost Gospel from Oxyrhynchus* (London: Henry Frowde; New York: Oxford University Press, 1904). These three fragmentary papyri, each of which comes from a different hand, were also published as part of the larger Oxyrhynchus find. POxy 1 appeared in *Oxyrhynchus Papyri 1* (London: Egypt Exploration Fund, 1898), 1–3; POxy 654 and 655 appeared in *Oxyrhynchus Papyri 4* (London: Egypt Exploration Fund, 1904), 1–28.

3. It was French scholar H.-Ch. Puech who made the connection that would pull these ancient fragments back into the limelight. Puech noticed

The *Gospel of Thomas* turned out not to be like the better-known gospels from the New Testament. Perhaps the most striking difference is that in this gospel there is no narrative to speak of. It tells no story of Jesus' life. Rather, it is simply a collection of Jesus' sayings, each introduced by the bare formula "Jesus says."

The one complete copy of the *Gospel of Thomas* we possess from Nag Hammadi has 114 such sayings. This copy, however, may not be identical to the original *Gospel of Thomas*. For one thing, it is a translation into Coptic of a more original, Greek version of this text, of which Grenfell and Hunt's Oxyrhynchus fragments are a reminder. Coptic is a written form of late Egyptian especially useful to the Christians who brought Christianity to Egypt in the second century. It uses the Greek alphabet (together with a few unique characters to represent the Egyptian sounds not found in Greek) to give expression to the native Egyptian language commonly spoken but rarely written during this period. Thus, our sole surviving complete copy of *Thomas* is actually a translation. The Greek fragments of *Thomas* discovered by Grenfell and Hunt are linguistically closer to the original. But the texts they represent were not identical to the Coptic version from Nag Hammadi. For example, one Greek fragment, POxy 1, lists Saying 30 and part of Saying 77 from the Coptic version in consecutive order. Another fragment, POxy 655, offers a version of Saying 36 that is much longer than the same saying in the Coptic text.

One of the reasons for such differences may be that the *Gospel of Thomas* is a sayings collection. As a simple

---

that the sayings of POxy 654 corresponded to the prologue and first seven sayings of the newly discovered Coptic *Gospel of Thomas*, the six sayings of POxy 1 to Sayings 28–33 (plus 77b), and the fragmentary sayings of POxy 655 to Sayings 24 and 36–39. See his "Une collection des paroles de Jésus récemment retrouvée: L'Evangile selon Thomas," in Académie des inscriptions et belles lettres, *Comptes rendus des séances de l'année 1957* (1957): 146–66; see also "The Gospel of Thomas," in E. Hennecke and W. Schneemelcher, *New Testament Apocrypha*, vol. 1, *Gospels and Related Writings* (Philadelphia: Westminster, 1963), 278–307.

collection, unlike the more complicated narrative texts of
the Bible, *Thomas* would have been much more malleable
and susceptible to change over the course of its transmission, as new sayings were added or sloughed off, expanded,
contracted, or shifted around as usefulness dictated. There
may have been many versions of the *Gospel of Thomas* at
one time or another. The three Oxyrhynchus fragments of
Thomas actually come from three different copies of the text
made at different times. The earliest of these (POxy 1) was
created early in the third century.[4] The Coptic version of
Thomas from Nag Hammadi was created early in the fourth
century.[5] Thus we know that Thomas enjoyed a long history
of popularity in upper Egypt. Over the course of this history,
and in the years it circulated prior to its arrival in Egypt, the
Gospel of Thomas was probably altered many times.

The *Gospel of Thomas,* as a sayings collection, was not
unique in the ancient world. In fact, such collections were
rather common. The students of well-known philosophers,
such as Epicurus or Epictetus, often collected the sayings of
their teachers into gnomologia, or collected words of insight,
which they might then use as they evangelized the public in
the market places and streets of the ancient city. This practice extended across cultures in antiquity. Jews, Egyptians,

---

4. Grenfell and Hunt dated it on the basis of the script and the level
at which it was discovered at Oxyrhynchus (see *Logia Iesou,* 6). Harry
Attridge dates it to shortly after 200 C.E. in his Introduction to the Greek
fragments of Thomas in B. Layton, ed., *Nag Hammadi Codex II,2–7, Together with XII,2, Brit. Lib. Or. 4926 (1), and P. Oxy 1, 654, 655,* vol. 1,
*Gospel According to Thomas, Gospel According to Philip, Hypostasis of
the Archons, and Indexes,* Nag Hammadi Studies 20 (Leiden: Brill, 1989),
97.

5. The Nag Hammadi codices are dated on the basis of the cartonnage
used in the manufacture of their bindings; see James M. Robinson, "Introduction," in *The Nag Hammadi Library in English* (1988, 1990, 1996, see
below, p. 93, n. 15), 16. Nag Hammadi Codex II has been dated by Søren
Giversen: "An absolute dating places it as contemporary with Br. M. Pap.
1920 and therefore from 330 to 340, or more loosely from the first half
of the fourth century" (*Apocryphon Johannis,* Acta Theologica Danica 5
[Copenhagen: Munksgaard, 1963], 40).

Persians, and other peoples of the Mediterranean basin also gathered the proverbial wisdom of their sages into collections of *logoi sophōn*, or sayings of the wise.[6] In the Jewish tradition one finds such collections embedded in, for example, the book of Proverbs or the intertestamental books of the Wisdom of Solomon and the Wisdom of Jesus ben Sirach. The gathering of Jesus' sayings into such a collection was therefore not a neutral activity. It placed *Thomas* among the great sages of Israel's history. He was, as the writer of the Wisdom of Solomon might have said, one of those holy souls found in each generation into whom the goddess Wisdom sends her spirit to make them friends of God and prophets (Wis. of Sol. 7:27).

2. Who Wrote the *Gospel of Thomas*?

The opening lines of the *Gospel of Thomas* read as follows:

> These are the hidden words that the living Jesus spoke.
> And Didymos Judas Thomas wrote them down.
>
> (*Thom.* Introduction)

The collection of these sayings is ascribed to a certain Didymos Judas Thomas, or in the Greek original (see POxy 654) simply "Judas, who is also called Thomas." This is a curious name. Only one part of it is a bona fide given name: Judas. Didymos is the Greek word for "twin" and Thomas the Semitic word. Originally the writer was identified as

---

6. The location of the *Gospel of Thomas* within the genre of *Logoi Sophōn,* or "sayings of the wise," was the contribution of James M. Robinson in his article, "*LOGOI SOPHŌN*: Zur Gattung der Spruchquelle," in E. Dinkler, ed., *Zeit und Geschichte. Dankesgabe an Rudolf Bultmann* (Tübingen: Mohr [Siebeck], 1964), 77–96; revised English translation, "*LOGOI SOPHŌN*: On the Gattung of Q," in idem and H. Koester, *Trajectories Through Early Christianity* (Philadelphia: Fortress, 1971), 71–113. Robinson's thesis was extended and explored more thoroughly by John S. Kloppenborg in *The Formation of Q: Trajectories in Ancient Wisdom Collections*, Studies in Antiquity and Christianity (Philadelphia: Fortress, 1987).

Judas Thomas (that is, Judas the Twin); later someone added the Greek word for twin for audiences unfamiliar with the Semitic word *thoma*. In any event, our purported scribe is Judas the Twin. Who was he?

Judas Thomas, or Judas the Twin, was a popular legendary figure from ancient Syrian Christianity. In the third-century *Acts of Thomas* (of Syrian origin), this "Judas Thomas, who is also called Didymus" is identified with the apostle Thomas. This may have been because the apostle Thomas was in some early Christian traditions also referred to as the Twin (see John 11:16; 14:5 [in some ancient manuscripts]; 20:24–28; 21:2). This connection between Judas Thomas and the apostle Thomas probably explains how it happened that the title of this gospel, which comes at the end of the text rather than the beginning (as is common for ancient tracts), was affixed as the Gospel According to *Thomas*, not the Gospel According to *Judas* Thomas.

But who was this Judas Thomas, or Judas the Twin? Judas the Twin appears in the Syriac version of the Gospel of John. There, John 14:22 identifies "Judas, who is not the Iscariot" as "Judas Thomas." This character also shows up obliquely in the Syrian *Acts of Thomas*. In *Acts Thom.* 11 Jesus appears in the guise of Thomas but explains, "I am not Judas who is also called Thomas, but his brother." So in this text, at any rate, Judas Thomas appears to have been a brother of Jesus. This, of course, calls to mind the curious fact that in Mark 6:3 we find named among the brothers of Jesus a certain "Judas." Could it be that the *Gospel of Thomas* intends to claim as its author Judas, the twin brother of Jesus?[7]

However one might assess this odd assembly of connections, it is clear that both the opening line and the title of the *Gospel of Thomas* intend to claim for its traditions the seal of ancient or apostolic authority. As with all such claims, they must be assessed critically. Anonymous or pseudonymous writings are far more common in the ancient world

---

7. Helmut Koester suggests this in his "Introduction (to the *Gospel of Thomas*)," in B. Layton, ed., *Nag Hammadi Codex II,2–7*, 1:39.

than texts written and signed by their actual authors, so that any ascription is automatically suspect. The slightly competing claims of the title (Thomas) and the opening line (Judas) also do not lend us confidence in identifying the author for this text. In any event, it is probably not reasonable to ascribe an ancient collection such as this to any one author. Over the years it may have had many curators, some of whom would have added new sayings upon learning of them, while others pared off outmoded material. It therefore seems best not to attach too much historical significance to the text's own authorial claims, and to assume that the collection was "authored" pseudonymously.

3. Where Was the *Gospel of Thomas* Written?

As we have seen, the name Judas Thomas, or Didymos Judas Thomas, is to be found primarily in early Christian texts associated with eastern Syria. To those already mentioned in which Judas Thomas plays a role, we might add the *Book of Thomas* and the Abgar legends, both of Syrian origin, and the sermons of the famous Syrian church father Ephraem, among others. Often in early Christianity, the name of a particularly prominent leader came to have significance within a distinct geographic region. Peter, for example, was associated with Rome, John with Asia Minor, James with Jerusalem, John Mark with Alexandria, and so forth. Whether such associations are grounded in a historical memory of the evangelization of that area or are purely legendary is difficult to say. Thomas, or Judas Thomas, was apparently the patron apostle for Syria. Thus it seems reasonable to assume that the *Gospel of Thomas* came originally out of Syria.[8]

---

8. Again, it was Puech who made the initial connection to Syria; see "The Gospel of Thomas," 287. In spite of problems with Puech's original suggestion, this has become the consensus. For a summary of the issues, see Stephen J. Patterson, *The Gospel of Thomas and Jesus* (Sonoma, Calif.: Polebridge, 1993), 118–20.

Yet, all of these Syrian sources in which we find evidence for the Judas Thomas tradition postdate the *Gospel of Thomas* by at least a century and more. This raises the question of whether the *Gospel of Thomas* was heir to the Syrian Thomas tradition or in fact predates it, perhaps even bearing some of the responsibility for bringing this tradition to Syria in the first place. After all, as a collection of Jesus' sayings, much of the material in the *Gospel of Thomas* would have emerged originally from the early Jesus movement in Palestine. Furthermore, *Thom.* 12 departs from the dominant tradition of appealing to Thomas for authority in this text and appeals instead to "James the Just," that is, James the brother of Jesus, who is thought to have been a leader in the early church in Jerusalem (see Gal. 1:19). Thus, it may be that the *Gospel of Thomas* was originally assembled not in Syria but further west, in Christian circles active in and around Jerusalem. Later it may have been transported to the east, where it became the basis for the subsequent flowering of the Thomas tradition in Syria.

4. When Was the *Gospel of Thomas* Written?

Thomas is difficult to date with any precision. The problem lies with the nature of the text itself: it is a sayings collection. As I have already indicated, this means that as a document *Thomas* would have been much more malleable than the better-known canonical gospels. It is this malleability that poses the greatest difficulty in reaching any consensus about when this text might have been written. The problem may be stated quite simply: a collection of sayings cannot be dated in the same way as a novel or treatise, where the creation of the whole composition in all its constituent parts might be located within a relatively limited time frame. In a sayings collection, such as *Thomas,* the sayings themselves might stem from disparate time periods, and may well have been introduced into the text over a long period of time. Therefore, one should probably not try to date *Thomas* in the same way that one might date a text like the Gospel of Mark. Rather, one should ask about the history of the *Gospel of Thomas:* When did it begin? How did it continue? Did it ever end?

When did it begin? There are several indications that some version of the *Gospel of Thomas* may have existed relatively early, before the end of the first century. First, the sayings collection as a literary form belongs to the earliest period of Christian literary activity, as evidenced by the so-called Synoptic Sayings Source, or Q (from the German *Quelle,* meaning "source"), a collection of sayings and parables used by Matthew and Luke in the composition of their gospels. Another, shorter example of this literary form may be the collection of parables found in Mark 4. The fate of these two examples of the genre is instructive: neither survived as an independent document; rather, both were absorbed into the more biographical genres favored by Christians in the latter part of the first century. This suggests that a climate developed in the later period of Christian origins that was not particularly hospitable to the sayings collection as an expression of Christian faith.[9] As one moves into the second century, the biography-like gospels such as one finds in the New Testament come more and more to dominate the scene. One may think also of the so-called Apostles' Creed that emerged only in the second century, completely lacking in sayings of Jesus and focussed only on his birth and death. To the extent that the sayings collection survived, it did so primarily among emerging Gnostic groups, which tended to recast it in the form of a dialogue between the resurrected Lord and his former students. This may explain why this genre was shunned by non-Gnostic Christian groups. At any rate, as a sayings collection, it is likely that *Thomas* originated sometime in the first century, when sayings collections had not yet given way to other, more complex forms of literature, such as the narrative story or dialogue.

An original date before the end of the first century is also

---

9. So Robinson, "*LOGOI SOPHŌN*," 113.

suggested by the way various authority figures appear in *Thomas*.[10] In *Thom.* 12, James is appealed to as an authority. In *Thom.* 13, another authority is lifted up: Thomas. Other apostles do not fare so well, however. In *Thom.* 13, Thomas is exalted but Peter and Matthew must play the fool, unable to understand the real significance and identity of Jesus. This suggests a time in early Christianity when local communities had begun to appeal to the authority of particular well-known leaders from the past to guarantee the reliability of their claims, even while rejecting the rival claims of others and their apostolic heroes. The rather pointed criticism of Matthew and Peter in *Thom.* 13 suggests that perhaps the author of this saying has in view the Gospel of Matthew and the particular form of Christianity associated with it. On the other hand, it has recently been argued that the rough treatment Thomas receives in John 20:24–29 is a direct attack on the *Gospel of Thomas* and the particular form of Christianity associated with it.[11] This sort of rivalry seems at home more in the first century than later. As apostolic history gradually faded into the distant past, such apostolic-inspired rivalries seem to have quieted — or shifted to other flashpoints — as all the apostles became revered figures of that remote time of sacred origins. Perhaps Luke made the first step in this direction. In Acts, written around the turn of the first century or perhaps slightly later,[12] the twelve apostles have become heroes of the early church, only a little less in stature than Jesus himself. And old rivalries, even as fierce as that which existed between Peter and Paul, are smoothed out. In Acts, Paul accepts the Jerusalem church's position on circumcision (Acts 16:3), and Peter accepts the Pauline position on eating with Gentiles (Acts 10). *Thomas*, with its raw

10. Koester, "Introduction," 40–41.

11. See Gregory Riley, *Resurrection Reconsidered: Thomas and John in Controversy* (Minneapolis: Fortress, 1995).

12. Helmut Koester, *Introduction to the New Testament*, vol. 2, *History and Literature of Early Christianity* (Berlin and New York: Walter de Gruyter; Philadelphia: Fortress, 1982), 310.

display of apostolic rivalries, probably originated before this period of accommodation.

Finally, there is the way that Jesus himself is treated in this collection. Throughout the collection one is hard pressed to find an instance in which Jesus is referred to by any of the Christological titles that became ever more prominent as the early followership of Jesus grew into a full-fledged religious movement.[13] He is not the "Son of Man,"[14] or the "Son of God,"[15] or the "Messiah" or "Christ," or even the "Lord."[16] He is just Jesus. Of course, the content of many sayings of *Thomas* implies a view of Jesus that was more exalted than this lack of Christological titles would suggest. Nonetheless, their absence is indicative of an earlier rather than later time frame.

All of this suggests that some form of the *Gospel of Thomas* existed already before the end of the first century. This does not mean, however, that everything we now see in this gospel derives from this early period. There is evidence that over time this gospel did indeed grow and change as newer sayings were added or older sayings altered. A good example of a newer saying is *Thom.* 7, a mysterious logion that reads as follows:

> [1] Jesus says: "Blessed is the lion that a person will eat and the lion will become human. [2] And anathema is the person whom a lion will eat and the lion will become human."

This odd image fits into the religious environment one finds among the ascetic monks of upper Egypt in the sec-

---

13. Koester, "Introduction," 40.

14. This term occurs in *Thom.* 86, but here it is probably not to be taken in the titular sense, but as the Semitic circumlocution for "human being."

15. The trinitarian formula in *Thom.* 44 may be an exception to this, though the formulation of this saying seems manifestly late.

16. This term occurs in *Thom.* 74, but it is not clear that it should be taken as referring to Jesus, or that it should be understood as titular in any case.

ond century and later, where the lion had come to symbolize
the human passions those ascetics fought to resist. It was
probably added to the collection some time after it had
come to Egypt and been adopted by Christian ascetics living
there.[17]

Other sayings in *Thomas* show how traditions that may
have been very old were nonetheless changed over the course
of their transmission under the influence of other texts and
traditions, such as the canonical gospels. A good instance of
this is to be found in *Thom.* 65–66. *Thom.* 65 is a version
of the parable of the tenants found also in Mark 12:1–12
and its parallels in Matthew and Luke. The *Thomas* version
is distinctive in that here the parable is a true parable; it
has not been secondarily allegorized as was the Markan version. In this sense, it derives ultimately from a stage in the
Jesus tradition that predates the Gospel of Mark. However,
even though *Thom.* 65 has none of the allegorical features
of Mark's more developed version, it is followed in the collection curiously by *Thom.* 66, a citation of Ps. 118:22. This
is the psalm text (plus verse 23) that Mark just happens to
append to his version of the parable (Mark 12:10b–11) to
complete his allegorical reading of it. For Mark, Jesus is the
rejected stone of the psalm. Since *Thomas* has no apparent
interest in reading the parable allegorically, there is no reason for the psalm to appear together with the parable in
Thomas. Indeed, in *Thomas* they are presented as separate
sayings, each introduced by "Jesus says," so that one is not
explicitly directed to read them together. Still, the location
of the psalm directly after the parable in Thomas seems to
be too much of a coincidence not to suppose that one of the
synoptic versions of this parable has exercised an influence
on the formation of the *Thomas* text.[18]

---

17. This is the hypothesis of Howard Jackson, whose study, *The Lion
Becomes Man: The Gnostic Leontomorphic Creator and the Platonic Tradition*, SBL Dissertation Series 81 (Atlanta: Scholars Press, 1985), has thus
far proven to be definitive for this saying.

18. For more on the problem of *Thom.* 65 and 66 see Patterson, *Gospel
of Thomas and Jesus*, 48–51. The relationship between *Thomas* and the

So not everything in the *Gospel of Thomas* comes from the first century. And not everything in *Thomas* that does come from this early period remained unchanged and free from the influence of other texts and traditions. As generations of scribes tinkered with and tweaked this tradition, influence from any number of directions would have exercised an effect on the text of *Thomas*. It is unlikely that we will be able to sort out all the intertextual possibilities with certainty. Thus, we must be content for now with a more general picture. The genesis of the *Gospel of Thomas* probably lies in the last decades of the first century, when sayings collections were still current, apostolic pedigrees were still disputed, and Jesus was still sometimes just "Jesus." But this collection grew and changed. Scribes were probably still adding and altering things when the Coptic version we now possess was copied in the fourth century by a monk in upper Egypt. The interpreter of *Thomas* must always hold open the possibility of various time frames for individual logia.[19]

---

synoptics is treated fully by Patterson, *Gospel of Thomas and Jesus,* 17–93. For a summary of other instances in *Thomas* where influence from the synoptic tradition is evident, see pp. 92–93. For a review of the extensive debate on this issue, see Stephen J. Patterson, "The Gospel of Thomas and the Synoptic Tradition: A Forschungsbericht and Critique," *Forum* 8, nos. 1–2 (1992): 45–97.

19. There is no consensus around this issue in the still lively debate. However, this sort of piecemeal approach has proven attractive to many as a reasonable way to proceed. Still, new proposals are in the offing that may add yet more clarity to the issue. Recently, for example, Hans-Martin Schenke has proposed on the basis of *Thom.* 68 that the *Gospel of Thomas* must have been written after the Bar Kochba rebellion in 135 c.e., when Jews were banished from Jerusalem by the Romans ("On the Compositional History of the Gospel of Thomas," *Forum* 10 [1994, appeared 1998]: 9–30). In his recent commentary, Richard Valantasis has suggested, based on common concerns he sees in John, Ignatius, and *Thomas,* a date just after the turn of the first century (*The Gospel of Thomas* [London and New York: Routledge, 1997], 12–21).

5. *Thomas* and Early Christian Social Radicalism

Early Christianity was a diverse phenomenon. From its very inception the followership of Jesus comprised disparate groups that came in various ways to understand Jesus as significant for their lives and, for many, determinative for their understanding of who God is. Based on what we read in the *Gospel of Thomas*, what can be said about the sort of Christianity (if one may rightly call such early Jesus people "Christians" at all) reflected there?

Those who used this gospel must have embraced an attitude about conventional life and the world around them that can only be described as socially radical. The *Thomas* Christians were not alone among the followers of Jesus in coming to this understanding of the significance of Jesus' life and teaching. In fact, in recent years the study of the synoptic gospels and their antecedent traditions has shown that among the earliest followers of Jesus it was common to find this sort of social radicalism. Gerd Theissen initiated the study of this aspect of the early Jesus movement and coined a term to describe it: *Wanderradikalismus,* or "wandering radicalism."[20] According to Theissen, the early Jesus movement was characterized by an itinerant lifestyle, imitating the itinerant life of Jesus himself. This is the origin and context within which such familiar sayings as this would have been remembered:

> [1] Jesus says, "[Foxes have] their holes and birds have their nest. [2] But the son of man has no place to lay his head down (and) to rest."
>
> (*Thom.* 86; cf. Matt. 8:20//Luke 9:58 [Q])

These early itinerants would have left behind conventional family life, of which they had become critical:

> [1] Jesus says: "Whoever does not hate his father and his mother cannot become a disciple of mine.

---

20. See, for example, his book *The Sociology of Early Palestinian Christianity,* trans. John Bowden (Philadelphia: Fortress, 1978).

²And whoever does not hate his brothers and his sisters (and) will not take up his cross as I do, will not be worthy of me."
(*Thom.* 55; cf. Matt. 10:37–38//Luke 14:26–27 [Q])

They would also have become critical of common piety, distinctions of clean and unclean, and purity as a means of validating human worth and belonging: "There is nothing outside a person that by going in can defile.... " (Mark 7:15; cf. Matt. 5:11; *Thom.* 14:5). And they embraced those who had fallen out of the mainstream of society into the realm of human expendability:

Jesus says: "Blessed are the poor. For the kingdom of heaven belongs to you."
(*Thom.* 54; cf. Matt. 5:3//Luke 6:20b [Q])

Blessed are you who hunger, for you will be satisfied.
(Matt. 5:6//Luke 6:21a [Q]; cf. *Thom.* 69:2)

Blessed are you when(ever) they hate you (and) persecute you.
(*Thom.* 68; cf. Matt. 5:10–11//Luke 6:22 [Q])

And they characterized wealth as useless:

¹Jesus says: "There was a rich person who had many possessions. ²He said: 'I will use my possessions so that I might sow, reap, plant, (and) fill my storehouses with fruit so that I will not lack anything.' ³This was what he was thinking in his heart. And in that night he died."
(*Thom.* 63:1–3; cf. Luke 12:16–20)

Or again:

¹[Jesus says:] "If you have money, do not lend (it) out at interest. ²Rather, give [it] to the one from whom you will not get it (back)."
(*Thom.* 95; cf. Matt. 5:42//Luke 6:30, 34–35 [Q])

But while this socially radical tradition is imbedded in the early Jesus tradition, it is also clear that by the time it was incorporated into the New Testament gospels, it had lost much of its edge. So, for example, when a rich young man comes to Jesus in the Gospel of Mark, but is sent away because he is unable to renounce his wealth and take up the itinerant life, we find this scenario:

> And [the disciples] were perplexed, wondering to themselves, "Well, then, who can be saved?" Jesus looks them in the eye and says, "For mortals it is impossible, but not with God; for everything is possible with God." (Mark 10:26–27; cf. Matt. 19:25–26; Luke 18:26–27)

In synoptic Christianity the early social radicalism of the Jesus movement gave way to a form of belonging that did not require the rigorous demands of itinerancy and world renunciation. This was perhaps inevitable if the movement of Jesus' followers was to escape the fate of so many other peripatetic philosophical movements that fell into obscurity and, eventually, extinction.

By scanning the citations listed above, one can see that the social radicalism that characterized the early synoptic tradition is also found in the *Gospel of Thomas*. But unlike the synoptic gospels, one does not find in *Thomas* any evidence to suggest that in *Thomas* circles this early radical tradition ever gave way to a more sedentary accommodation of it. This means that both synoptic and *Thomas* Christianity have their origins in an early, socially radical Jesus movement. But while synoptic Christianity followed a trajectory that led to a more settled community life, *Thomas* Christianity continued on a trajectory of itinerant social radicalism. The legacy of this socially radical tradition, with its benchmarks of itinerancy and voluntary poverty, can be seen in the character of Christianity as it developed in eastern Syria, where the *Thomas* tradition eventually found its home. Syrian Christianity always maintained a strongly ascetical flavor, and itinerant monks were part of the Syrian Christian landscape for centuries.[21]

---

21. For a more complete discussion of these historical developments, see Patterson, *Gospel of Thomas and Jesus*, 121–95.

6. The Theology of the *Gospel of Thomas*

How did *Thomas* Christians think about their socially radical stance? What did they think of the world and their place in it that would have sustained their will to remain outside the mainstream of social life? What was their view of Jesus? What can be said about *Thomas* theology?

Let us begin with the fact that the *Gospel of Thomas* is a sayings collection. As we have already noted, this places *Thomas* within a well-used genre of ancient literature — *logoi sophōn*, "words of the wise" or "sayings of the sages," as James M. Robinson has called it. The use of this genre has implications that extend beyond its merely formal characteristics. It comes with an interpretive context: wisdom theology. The questions that occupied the cultivators of ancient Jewish wisdom theology were simple ones: What is the world like? What are people like? What is wise and prudent? Who am I, and what is my place in the larger scheme of things? These are simple questions, and sometimes they can be answered simply. Wisdom literature abounds in simple, proverbial statements of observable truth. For example, this well-known proverb is straightforwardly prudent:

> Jesus says: "If a blind (person) leads a blind (person), both will fall into a pit." (*Thom.* 34)

But sometimes these simple questions of life are not so simply answered. What if, for example, one's experience of the world is not conventional? What if one feels alienated or out of place in the world? What if through various circumstances one has come to view the world differently from most, as a strange and hostile place? Many Christians came to view the world in this way, partly because Jesus had fared so poorly in it. The apostle Paul says, for example:

> Yet among the mature we do impart wisdom, although it is not a wisdom of this age or of the rulers of this age, who are doomed to pass away. But we impart a secret and hidden wisdom of God, which God decreed

before the ages for our glorification. None of the rulers
of this age understood this; for if they had, they would
not have killed the Lord of glory.   (1 Cor. 2:6–8)

The *Gospel of Thomas* shares this negative attitude toward
the world. In fact, the very next words from Paul's pen in
the passage just cited are a saying found also in the *Gospel
of Thomas*:

But, as it is written, "What no eye has seen, nor ear
heard, nor the human heart conceived, what God has
prepared for those who love him," God has revealed to
us through the Spirit.   (1 Cor. 2:9; cf. *Thom.* 17)

What *Thomas* and Paul share is the conviction that the
world is not as it seems. To know it — to really know it as
it is — one must attend not to conventional wisdom but to
the true wisdom that is revealed from God. In the *Gospel of
Thomas* Jesus is the bearer of such revelation. Of the world
he says:

[1] "Whoever has come to know the world has found a
corpse. [2] And whoever has found (this) corpse, of him
the world is not worthy."   (*Thom.* 56)

Or again:

Jesus says: "The one who has found the world (and) has
become wealthy should renounce the world."

(*Thom.* 110)

Or:

[3] Does not Jesus say: "Whoever has found himself, of
him the world is not worthy"?   (*Thom.* 111:3)

Finally:

[1] "If you do not abstain from the world, you will not
find the kingdom."   (*Thom.* 27:1)

The *Gospel of Thomas* does not hold the world in high es-
teem. It is an evil place, or rather, a dead and inferior place,

unworthy of the followers of Jesus, who have the misfortune to dwell in it. How does one come to understand the world in such terms? For Paul, it was that he, like Jesus, experienced the world as hostile to the utopian vision he had gained from Christianity and was now working toward, indeed, expecting to come in fullness any day at God's initiative, with Jesus leading the way as the returning Son of Man. Paul gave expression to his frustration with the world by embracing an apocalyptic world view.

Thomas Christians did not think this way. Instead, they embraced a world view more akin to what one finds in the Gospel of John. John's view of the world was also hostile: "If the world hates you, know that it hated me before it hated you," says Jesus to his disciples in the "Farewell Discourse" (John 15:18). And so Jesus departs from the world to go to another place, where his followers too will someday go:

> In my Father's house are many rooms. If it were not so I would have told you. I go now to prepare a place for you. And when I go and prepare a place for you, I will come again and will take you to myself, that where I am you may be also.   (John 14:2–3)

This is very much like the view we find in *Thomas.* In *Thomas,* too, Jesus appears as one who has come to redeem his followers to another world. Just as John's Jesus comes into a world that "received him not" (John 1:11), so also Jesus is disappointed in the *Gospel of Thomas:*

> [1] Jesus says: "I stood in the middle of the world, and in flesh I appeared to them. [2] I found all of them drunk. None of them did I find thirsty. [3] And my soul ached for the children of humanity, because they are blind in their heart, and they cannot see; for they came into the world empty, (and) they also seek to depart from the world empty. [4] But now they are drunk. (But) when they shake off their wine, then they will change their mind."
>
> (*Thom.* 28)

Like John's Jesus, Jesus in *Thomas* is here but for a brief time. He sojourns in the world, shares his words of divine wisdom, but ultimately must return to the heavenly abode from whence he has come. In John 7:33–34 Jesus says:

I will be with you a little longer, and then I will go to the one who sent me; you will seek me and you will not find me; where I am you will not be able to come.

Compare this to Jesus' words in *Thom.* 38:

[1] Jesus says: "Many times you have desired to hear these words, these that I am speaking to you, and you have no one else from whom to hear them.
[2] There will be days when you will seek me, (and) you will not find me."

And finally, as with Jesus in John, in *Thomas,* Jesus promises that someday his followers will return to their place of origin. They will not stay in the world of evil and corruption, but shall someday return to God:

[1] Jesus says: "Blessed are the solitary ones, the elect. For you will find the kingdom. [2] For you come from it (and) will return to it."   (*Thom.* 49)

In John this will happen as an answer to Jesus' prayer on behalf of the disciples (John 17). Not so in *Thomas*. In *Thomas* the followers of Jesus must know what to say and when to say it in order to identify themselves as those who truly are chosen, who really do come from God. As the saying just cited continues, it seems to join with the next saying to form a brief catechism for how one should respond to the powers that be as one makes one's way out of the world and back to the heavenly "Father":

[1] Jesus says: "If they say to you: 'Where do you come from?' (then) say to them: 'We have come from the light, the place where the light has come into being by itself, has established [itself] and has appeared in their image.'

²If they say to you: 'Is it you?' (then) say: 'We are his children, and we are the elect of the living Father.'

³If they ask you: 'What is the sign of your Father among you?' (then) say to them: 'It is movement and repose.' " (*Thom.* 50)

This basic idea — that Jesus is the redeemer come from God into a hostile and evil world to rescue a stranded race of chosen ones — is akin to an ancient religious movement that found expression in many different religions of the ancient orient, known as Gnosticism. Gnostics believed that the world was an evil place because it was created so by an evil demiurge who broke away from the one true God in an act of rebellion. In that act of creation he (or she) mixed that which is divine and spiritual with that which is evil and material. Those who possess some of that which is spiritual — a divine spark, if you will — form a special class of persons. Their true spiritual selves are mired in the material world, drowsy, drunk, forgetful of who they really are and where they have come from. But when the redeemer comes and speaks a word of truth — the knowledge (*gnosis*) of who they really are — they remember, awaken from their slumber, and long once again to return to their heavenly home to be reunited with the one true God.

Whether and to what extent Gnosticism influenced Christian texts such as the Gospel of John and the *Gospel of Thomas* has long been a matter of debate. Some of the elements of Gnosticism seem apparent enough: the negative view of the world, the depiction of persons as lost and weighed down by the world, the presentation of a redeemer figure who has descended from God, and the hoped for heavenly redemption of the souls of those who listen to the redeemer are all part of Gnosticism. But these things are not unique to Gnosticism. They are also found in speculative Jewish wisdom theology, such as one finds in the Alexandrian Jewish theologian Philo in the middle of the first century.[22] They are also present among Jewish and Chris-

---

22. Stevan Davies argues that this is the religious environment that best

tian mystics, who practiced asceticism and cultivated the visionary experience of ascent into the heavenly realms to behold the glory (*kavod*) of God.[23] Moreover, some of the most characteristic features of Gnosticism are not present in *Thomas*, such as the notion that the world was created by an evil demiurge, or that humanity itself is divided among those who share a divine origin (and so may be saved) and those who are simply material in nature (and thus lie beyond hope). These themes are developed in great detail and variety in later Gnostic tractates from the second century and later; in *Thomas* they are not present at all.

It is probably not as important to resolve the theoretical question of which category — wisdom, mysticism, Gnosticism — best contains all the ideas we see in the *Gospel of Thomas* as it is to understand the general religious milieu within which the theology of the *Gospel of Thomas* grew up. Gnosticism, Hellenistic Jewish wisdom speculation, and mysticism are all closely related phenomena in the religious world of antiquity.[24] Many people in the ancient Orient experienced the world as a foreign and brutal place. War, slavery, economic marginality, not to mention famine and disease, were part of most people's everyday experience. In such a world, many people came to the conclusion that God

---

explains *Thomas;* see his book *The Gospel of Thomas and Christian Wisdom* (New York: Seabury, 1983), and his essay, "The Christology and Protology of the *Gospel of Thomas,*" *Journal of Biblical Literature* 111 (1992): 663–92.

23. April de Conick argues that this is the religious environment that best explains *Thomas;* see her monograph *Seek to See Him: Ascent and Vision Mysticism in the Gospel of Thomas,* Supplements to Vigiliae Christianae (Leiden: E. J. Brill, 1996).

24. For the close connection between Gnosticism and speculative Jewish wisdom theology, see Hans-Martin Schenke, "Die Tendenz der Weisheit zur Gnosis," in B. Aland, ed., *Gnosis: Festschrift Hans Jonas* (Göttingen: Vandenhoeck & Ruprecht, 1978), 351–72. For the relationship between Gnosticism and Jewish mysticism see, e.g., G. Quispel, "Ezekiel 1:26 in Jewish Mysticism and Gnosis," *Vigiliae christianae* 34 (1980): 1–13, or J.-P. Mahé, "La Voie d'Immortalité à la lumière des *Hermetica* de Nag Hammadi et des Découvertes plus Récentes," *Vigiliae christianae* 45 (1991): 347–75.

lies above and beyond this morass, and that they too could rise above it and the hopeless suffering it seemed inevitably to offer. This is how *Thomas* Christians were beginning to think about things. They had come to the conclusion that the world was an inferior place, but they were ultimately not part of it. So they began to seek a way out.

In the *Gospel of Thomas* salvation is achieved through insight into Jesus' words. This is the basic hermeneutical framework of this gospel:

> And he said: "Whoever finds the meaning of these words will not taste death." (*Thom.* 1)

As the opening lines of the gospel continue, the idea that salvation may be gained through insight is expanded upon. The quest for insight is not easy; it must be pursued, contested. But for one who prevails in the search, great rewards are assured:

> [1] Jesus says: "The one who seeks should not cease seeking until he finds. [2] And when he finds, he will be dismayed. [3] And when he is dismayed, he will be astonished. [4] And he will be king over the All."
> (*Thom.* 2)

This is the Coptic version of *Thom.* 2. To the image of "reigning" in the final line, the Greek version of this saying adds "and he will rest." Seeking in order to find, the quest for insight, and the reward of the successful quester with "reign" and "rest" are concepts familiar from the religious world of Gnosticism and speculative Jewish wisdom theology. Here we encounter the idea that salvation is not just a future state to be found in the hereafter. Salvation begins now, in the present, as one begins to understand the divine words of insight. Just so, *Thomas* continues:

> [1] Jesus says: "If those who lead you say to you: 'Look, the kingdom is in the sky!' then the birds of the sky will precede you.

²If they say to you: 'It is in the sea,' then the fishes will precede you. ³Rather, the kingdom is inside of you and outside of you."

⁴"When you come to know yourselves, then you will be known, and you will realize that you are the children of the living Father. ⁵But if you do not come to know yourselves, then you exist in poverty and you are poverty."   (*Thom.* 3)

Notice where this saying places the locus of salvation: "you." "You" must know yourself; if not, "you" are the poverty. This is a very different understanding of salvation than that found in many New Testament writings and, thus, more familiar to most Christians today. *Thomas* Christians did not look to Jesus' death and resurrection as the key to salvation, nor even to Jesus himself as a savior. This is underscored by the fact, already noted above, that *Thomas* lacks Christological titles: Jesus is always simply "Jesus." Rather, *Thomas* Christians looked to Jesus' *words* and the insight that could be derived from them as the key to salvation. The goal is not to be saved by Jesus, but to become like Jesus, knowing what he knows. The following brief scene from *Thomas* illustrates this point. It is strongly reminiscent of Mark 8:27–30, where Jesus asks the disciples, "Who do people say that I am?" Mark's well-known scene culminates in Peter's correct identification of Jesus as the "Christ." Not so in Thomas:

¹Jesus said to his disciples: "Compare me and tell me whom I am like."

²Simon Peter said to him: "You are like a just messenger."

³Matthew said to him: "You are like an (especially) wise philosopher."

⁴Thomas said to him: "Teacher, my mouth cannot bear at all to say whom you are like."

⁵Jesus said: "I am not your teacher. For you have drunk, you have become intoxicated at the bubbling spring that I have measured out."   (*Thom.* 13:1–5)

The point in *Thomas* is not to arrive at a confession of who Jesus is, but to drink from the same waters from which Jesus himself has drunk and to begin to think like he thinks. Again:

> ¹Jesus says: "Whoever will drink from my mouth will become like me. ²I myself will become he ³and what is hidden will be revealed to him." (*Thom.* 108)

Where do these ideas come from? They are not foreign to early Christianity. Again, in the Gospel of John Jesus speaks in terms very similar to this. There, too, Jesus' words are "spirit and life" (John 6:63); any one who keeps his word "will never taste death" (John 8:51). To the Samaritan woman Jesus says, "Whoever drinks the water that I shall give will never thirst again; the water I shall give them will become in them a spring of water welling up to eternal life" (John 4:14).

But even earlier, in Q, one finds ideas strikingly similar to these. In Q the focus must also have been on Jesus' words, albeit from a perspective more practical and less speculative (see Luke 6:46–49; Matt. 7:21, 24–27 [Q]). But here, too, Jesus appears in his role as a revealer of divine truth:

> In that same hour [Jesus] rejoiced in the Holy Spirit and said, "I thank you, Father, Lord of heaven and earth, that you have hidden these things from the wise and the understanding and revealed them to babes; yes, Father, for this was your gracious will. All things have been delivered to me by my Father; and no one knows who the Son is except the Father, or who the Father is except the Son and anyone to whom the Son chooses to reveal him. (Luke 10:21–22; Matt. 11:25–27 [Q])

The similarities one can see between the ideas found in the *Gospel of Thomas* and ideas current in the Pauline communities, in Q, and in John show that we are dealing with an understanding of Jesus that was not foreign to earliest Christianity.[25] But in *Thomas* we find them in a combination that does not exist anywhere else. Thus, *Thomas* Christianity was distinctive, like many other early Christian groups, and so can be seen as contributing generally to the *diversity* of early Christian theology we are coming more and more to see as characteristic of earliest Christianity.[26]

---

25. For more on the relationship between *Thomas* Christianity and Paul see Stephen J. Patterson, "Paul and the Jesus Tradition: It Is Time for Another Look," *Harvard Theological Review* 84 (1991): 23–41. For more on Q and *Thomas,* see Stephen J. Patterson, "Wisdom in Q and Thomas," in Leo G. Perdue, Bernard Brandon Scott, and William Johnston Wiseman, eds., *In Search of Wisdom: Essays in Honor of John Gammie* (Louisville: (Westminster/John Knox, 1993), 187–221. For more on the relationship between John and *Thomas,* see Raymond Brown, "The Gospel of Thomas and St. John's Gospel," *New Testament Studies* 9 (1962/63): 155–77; more recently, see Gregory Riley, *Resurrection Reconsidered: Thomas and John in Controversy* (Minneapolis: Fortress, 1995).

26. The contribution *Thomas* makes to our understanding of the diversity of early Christianity was explored in the pioneering work of Helmut Koester in a series of articles. See especially, "GNOMAI DIAPHOROI: The Origin and Nature of Diversification in the History of Early Christianity," *Harvard Theological Review* 58 (1965): 279–318, reprinted in idem and James M. Robinson, *Trajectories,* 114–57; and "One Jesus and Four Primitive Gospels," *Harvard Theological Review* 61 (1968): 203–47, also reprinted in *Trajectories,* 158–204. On this general theme one should also consult Robinson's contributions to *Trajectories,* especially "LOGOI SOPHŌN" and "Kerygma and History in the New Testament,'" 20–70. More recently the issue of diversity in early Christianity has been pressed by Burton Mack in *A Myth of Innocence: Mark and Christian Origins* (Philadelphia: Fortress, 1988) and Ron Cameron in his essays, "Alternate Beginnings — Different Ends: Eusebius, Thomas, and the Construction of Christian Origins," in L. Bormann, K. del Tredici, and A. Standhartinger, eds., *Religious Propaganda and Missionary Competition in the New Testament World: Essays Honoring Dieter Georgi,* Novum Testamentum Supplements 74 (Leiden: Brill, 1994), 502–25, and "The Gospel of Thomas and Christian Origins,"in Birger A. Pearson, ed., *The Future of Early Christianity: Essays in Honor of Helmut Koester* (Minneapolis: Fortress, 1991), 381–92. All of these scholars are to some extent influenced by the pioneering work of Walter Bauer, *Orthodoxy and Heresy in Earliest Christianity,* ed. Robert A. Kraft and Gerhard Krodel, trans. Philadelphia Seminar on Christian Origins (Philadelphia: Fortress, 1971; originally published in German in 1934).

7. The *Gospel of Thomas*, Asceticism, and Mysticism

Thomas Christians viewed the world as an inferior place. They gave expression to this view in the way they lived and in how they thought. But is there evidence in *Thomas* to indicate that they expressed their disdain for the world in terms of their personal piety as well? Were they ascetics? Were they mystics? To get at this issue, we must first back up and understand something more about anthropology in the speculative theological discourse we have just been describing.

In all its various forms (Gnosticism, Hellenistic Jewish wisdom theology, Jewish mysticism) this speculative theology contained a heavy element of Platonic (or neo-Platonic) dualism. That is, those who cultivated these traditions thought of a human being as a mixture of material and spiritual elements. The material part of a person was thought to be connected closely to the material world, and thus subject to the corruption to which the Platonists believed the material world was prone. In this way the material element in a person was considered inferior to the spiritual element, whose origin, by contrast, was believed to lie in the divine godhead itself. It was necessary, therefore, to shed the material body in order that the spiritual element might be released and reascend to the heavens and be reunited with its divine source. For some, this problem of the body was solved very simply through death. Though one must struggle in life to resist the corrupting influence of the flesh and the world of which it is a part, eventually death will free the spiritual kernel from its material husk. But for others, this matter of freedom from the material world was more difficult. The struggle against the flesh and the material world must be enjoined; freedom from its corruption must be won through the discipline of asceticism and mysticism.

In the *Gospel of Thomas* there is a close connection between the body and the world for which *Thomas* Christians felt so much disdain. We noted above, in connection with the anti-cosmic stance of *Thomas*, the following saying:

> [1] Jesus says: "Whoever has come to know the world has found a corpse. [2] And whoever has found (this) corpse, of him the world is not worthy." (*Thom. 56*)

This strange, enigmatic saying has a doublet in *Thomas* — a twin — that is equally paradoxical. It reads as follows:

> [1] Jesus says: "Whoever has come to know the world has found the (dead) body. [2] But whoever has found the (dead) body, of him the world is not worthy."
> (*Thom. 80*)

Rather than simply exploring the nature of the world, these sayings are more interested in the connection between the world and the body. In the first half of the saying the two are equated: to know one is to know the other. If discovering the truth about the world means discovering its inferior nature, then one must conclude that one is encouraged to make a similar discovery about the body itself: like the world, it too is inferior — a mere corpse. But what of the second half of the saying? It simply follows upon the first: once one has discovered the true nature of the body, one can rise above it and the world. The world is no longer worthy of one who possesses such knowledge.

The *Gospel of Thomas* expresses disdain for the body of flesh just as it does for the material world. In *Thom.* 29 this disdain is expressed in terms of the dichotomy of flesh and spirit:

> [1] Jesus says: "If the flesh came into being because of the spirit, it is a wonder. [2] But if the spirit (came into being) because of the body, it is a wonder of wonders."

Here *Thomas*'s Jesus expresses his wonderment at how something so precious as the spirit has come to be joined with something so worthless as the body of flesh. The spirit and the flesh are seen as separate components, joined in an unholy mix, a conjunction that spells doom for both:

[1] Jesus says: "Woe to the flesh that depends on the soul.
[2] Woe to the soul that depends on the flesh."

(*Thom.* 112)

Such texts as these have usually been taken as evidence that those who used the *Gospel of Thomas* engaged in some form of asceticism.[27] Certainly this gospel would have given aid and comfort to early Christian ascetics, which may account for its presence in upper Egypt, a center of early Christian ascetic activity, in the first place.[28] However, when one scans the *Gospel of Thomas*, it is difficult to find clear, direct instructions referring to ascetic practice. Fasting is discussed, but on one occasion it is discouraged (along with the other pillars of early Jewish piety):

[1] Jesus said to them: "If you fast, you will bring forth sin for yourselves. [2] And if you pray, you will be condemned. [3] And if you give alms, you will do harm to your spirits." (*Thom.* 14:1–3)

Fasting is mentioned again in *Thom.* 104:

[1] They said to [Jesus]: "Come, let us pray and fast today!"
[2] Jesus said: "What sin is it that I have committed, or wherein have I been overcome? [3] But when the bridegroom comes out of the wedding chamber, then let (us) fast and pray."

Initially the saying seems to be in agreement with *Thom.* 14:1–2 in rejecting fasting and prayer. One is reminded here of the tradition in which Jesus is accused of being "a glutton and a drunkard" (see Luke 7:34; Matt. 11:19 [Q]). But then 104:3 seems to shift the position of the text: at some

---

27. See, for example, Richard Valantasis, *The Gospel of Thomas* (London and New York: Routledge, 1997), 21–24, et passim.

28. It may be that the organizing principle of the Nag Hammadi Library as a whole was asceticism, not Gnosticism, as was once thought. See Frederik Wisse, "Gnosticism and Early Monasticism in Egypt," in B. Aland, ed., *Gnosis: Festschrift Hans Jonas* (Göttingen: Vandenhoeck & Ruprecht, 1978), 431–40.

point fasting will be appropriate. But when? Does the "bridal chamber" refer to that ritual of initiation known from Syrian and later Gnostic Christianity? Could it be that although Jesus did not fast, here initiates into *Thomas* Christianity are encouraged to do so? Or does *Thom.* 104:3 refer in some enigmatic way to the death of Jesus (cf. the parallel tradition in Mark 2:20), so that one may fast after Jesus' death? Perhaps. Still, fasting is not uncommon as a pious practice; even if it is somehow encouraged in 104:3, this is hardly indicative of a full-scale asceticism among *Thomas* Christians.

If *Thomas* Christians were not ascetics in the stereotypical sense most people have in mind in using this term, they were certainly setting the stage for later, more ascetic forms of Christianity such as one finds in Syria and Egypt. The tradition of social radicalism that *Thomas* bears from the earliest Jesus tradition would have been a firm foundation for the wandering ascetics of later Syrian Christianity.[29] And the anti-cosmic ideology of *Thomas* would have formed the framework for ascetical withdrawal from the world.

Yet another set of texts in *Thomas* may have been useful to the self-understanding of those engaged in ascetical practices. *Thom.* 22 is perhaps the best representative of these sayings, which focus on the concept of the "image":

> [1] Jesus saw infants being suckled.
> [2] He said to his disciples: "These little ones being suckled are like those who enter the kingdom."
> [3] They said to him: "Then will we enter the kingdom as little ones?"
> [4] Jesus said to them: "When you make the two into one and when you make the inside like the outside and the outside like the inside and the above like the below — [5] that is, to make the male and the female into a single one, so that the male will not be male and the female will not be female — [6] and when you make eyes

---

29. See Patterson, *Gospel of Thomas and Jesus,* 163–68.

instead of an eye and a hand instead of a hand and a foot instead of a foot, an image instead of an image, [7]then you will enter [the kingdom]."

Of central importance in this saying are the ideas about the construction of self that come to expression in 22:4–6. How is it that one might remake oneself and become like an infant? One reconciles in oneself a series of oppositions: inside/outside, above/below, male/female. And one replaces one's own body with a new one: eye, hand, foot, and eventually one's whole image is replaced. How? The text does not say. But recent theoretical discussions of asceticism have suggested that this sort of remaking of the self — the creation of a new "subjectivity" — is what ascetical practice is all about.[30] That is why the ascetic focuses on the body: it is the tangible, reconstructable self.

Finally, there are sayings in the *Gospel of Thomas* that relate ascetic practice to visionary experiences of God. One of these we have already mentioned above as an illustration of *Thomas* Christians' attitude toward the world. It is repeated here, but now in full:

[1]"If you do not abstain from the world, you will not find the kingdom.

[2]If you do not make the Sabbath into a Sabbath, you will not see[31] the Father." (*Thom.* 27)

---

30. See Richard Valantasis, "Constructions of Power in Asceticism," *Journal of the American Academy of Religion* 63 (1995): 775–821; also "Adam's Body: Uncovering Esoteric Tradition in the *Apocryphon of John* and Origen's *Dialogue with Heraclides,*" *The Second Century* 7 (1990): 150–62. On this saying see Valantasis, *Gospel of Thomas*, 95–96.

31. That the text in fact reads "see" at this point has been disputed by Gregory Riley in "A Note on the Text of Gospel of Thomas 27," *Harvard Theological Review* 88 (1995): 179–81. Riley argues that the manuscript, somewhat fragmented here, actually reads *ney* ("to come") not *nay* ("to see"). Upon reexamination of the original manuscript, however, Marvin Meyer concludes in a forthcoming note to be published in the *Harvard Theological Review* that Riley is incorrect, misled by the black background of the photograph not having been fully painted out by the printer in Stuttgart.

Here asceticism is recommended as a kind of preparation for "seeing the Father." What might this mean, "seeing the Father"? It may refer to a kind of mysticism wherein one achieves a beatific vision of God. Such visionary, or mystical experiences were common among Jewish holy ones in the period of Christian origins and became part of early Christian religious practice as well.[32] Perhaps the best known Jewish Christian mystic is the apostle Paul, who, in 2 Cor. 12:2–4, makes oblique reference to his own ascent to the third heaven, to "Paradise" itself, where he "heard things that cannot be told, that a person may not utter." In any event, there are sayings in *Thomas* that indicate that those who used this text may have enjoyed a rich life of mystical experience. In *Thom.* 15, for example, those who would ascend to heaven to behold the face of God are instructed in the proper posture to take when encountering God:

> Jesus says: "When you see one who was not born of woman, fall on your face (and) worship him. That one is your Father."

Thom. 83 probably also has to do with instruction on what to look for when one encounters God in the beatific vision. It deals with the theme of "light," or the experience of luminosity that is often associated with visionary experience. In distinction from the light that is hidden within the human likeness, God's light is overwhelming:

> [1] Jesus says: "The images are visible to humanity, but the light within them is hidden in the image.
> [2] The light of the Father will reveal itself, but his image is hidden by his light."

There are probably other sayings in *Thomas* that are related to the ancient tradition of ascent mysticism, whereby

---

32. Sometimes known as *merkavah* mysticism, the phenomenon is best-described by Gershom Scholem in his classic study *Major Trends in Jewish Mysticism*, rev. ed. (New York: Schocken, 1946). See also his *Jewish Gnosticism, Merkabah Mysticism and Talmudic Tradition,* 2d ed. (New York: Jewish Theological Seminary, 1965).

disciplined asceticism was used to induce intense religious experiences of ascent into the heavens to behold the glory of God.[33] This, too, was part of the religious environment of this mysterious, eclectic gospel.

8. *Thomas* and Early Christianity

Where does *Thomas* fit into the overall landscape of early Christianity? As we have seen, the *Gospel of Thomas* represents a unique form of early Christian faith, but one that is not completely isolated from other versions of Christianity current in the first century. We have thus argued that *Thomas* contributes generally to our understanding of Christian origins as a diverse phenomenon encompassing many different strands of religious thought current in the ancient world.

This view, however, has not gone undisputed in the history of *Thomas* scholarship. In the early years of the discussion, many took the position that the *Gospel of Thomas* belonged not to first-century but second-century Christianity, and represented a late, corrupted form of Christian faith whose more original form was to be seen in the canonical gospels. This view of *Thomas* was undergirded by three interlocking assumptions, none of which seems warranted today. The first was that *Thomas* should be dated in the second century. The second was that *Thomas* was dependent on the synoptic gospels, and so should be seen as a late, secondarily derived form of Christian reflection. The third was that the

---

33. Recently April de Conick (*Seek to See Him*) has argued that ascent mysticism stands behind such sayings as *Thom.* 49, 50, 84, 82, 108, 13, 3, 67, 56, 80, 59, and 37. In many cases her arguments are quite convincing and illuminating. However, she is mistaken in her juxtaposition of mysticism to Gnosticism and in reaching the conclusion that the *Gospel of Thomas* is a mystic's gospel, not a Gnostic's. Mysticism and Gnosticism are in no way incompatible, as a text like the *Three Steles of Seth* from Nag Hammadi, a kind of Gnostic ascent liturgy, clearly shows. The mystic's ascent in such cases may be seen as a kind of liturgical dress rehearsal for that day when the soul will once and for all depart to be reunited with the divine godhead.

Gnostic ideas in *Thomas* belong in the second century, where Gnosticism first emerged as an early Christian heresy.

We have already seen that *Thomas* should not necessarily be dated in the second century. Advocates for a second-century date have sometimes appealed to Grenfell and Hunt, who speculated that if POxy 654, the earliest of the Greek fragments of *Thomas,* was created just after 200 C.E., then the original of this text could have been composed no later than 140 C.E. This *terminus ad quem* has often been cited as their date for Thomas. But note that this was their estimate of the *latest* possible date, not the *earliest*. With the whole *Gospel of Thomas* now in front of us we are in a position to revise this view, as I have attempted to do above (see pp. 40–45), suggesting a series of reasons for positing an original composition in the last decades of the first century, but allowing for much growth and change over the long course of its history.

The second assumption, that *Thomas* was dependent on the synoptic gospels, received an enormous amount of attention in the early years of the *Thomas* debate — and still does today. It is obviously a basic issue in locating *Thomas* within early Christianity. Proponents of the view that *Thomas* was dependent on the synoptic gospels have based their position on the several occasions where the *Thomas* version of a saying seems to reflect the editorial work of one or another of the synoptic evangelists. This could only mean that the author of *Thomas* had copied such sayings from the synoptic text itself.[34] There are indeed several places where this ap-

---

34. For a discussion of this view and its proponents see Patterson, "Thomas and the Synoptic Tradition," 50–63, 79–82. The most thorough attempt to prove *Thomas*'s dependence in this way was that of W. Schrage, *Das Verhältnis des Thomas-Evangeliums zur synoptischen Tradition und zu den koptischen Evangelienübersetzungen. Zugleich ein Beitrag zur gnostischen Synoptikerdeutung*, Beihefte zur Zeitschrift für die neutestamentliche Wissenschaft 29 (Berlin: Töpelmann, 1964). But Schrage's failure to consider the implications of redaction critical analysis in his study, and his unwarranted assumption that influence at the level of the Coptic translations would necessarily mean dependence at the point

pears to be true.[35] But taken together, these instances do not suggest any consistent pattern of borrowing. And they are far outnumbered by the many sayings that show no knowledge at all of their synoptic counterparts, and in many cases appear to come from a stage in the tradition that is more primitive. In one instance (POxy 655, Saying 36) *Thomas* seems to have preserved a sayings cluster in a form that is older than the form found in Q, since it has not undergone the scribal editing found in Q, and even lacks a scribal error present already in Q.[36] This, together with the fact that roughly half of *Thomas*'s sayings have no parallels with the synoptic tradition at all, indicates that *Thomas* represents a stream of tradition that is basically autonomous and distinct from the synoptic tradition. As years passed, intertextual

---

of original composition, left his work deeply flawed. Among the recent, more thoughtful treatments from this point of view is the study by C. M. Tuckett, "Thomas and the Synoptics," *Novum Testamentum* 30 (1988): 132–57. Tuckett proposes a saying-by-saying approach, refusing to rule out any possibilities prematurely.

35. In *Gospel of Thomas and Jesus* (pp. 17–99) my own analysis unearthed several such places, including *Thom.* 32 (cf. Matt. 5:14b); *Thom.* 39:1–2 (cf. Matt. 23:13); *Thom.* 45:2–4 (cf. Luke 6:45); *Thom.* 104:1 (cf. Luke 5:33); and *Thom.* 104:3 (cf. Luke 5:33–35). There are also a few places where the order of sayings in *Thomas* seems to have been influenced by the synoptic gospels, including *Thom.* 32 and 33:2–3; *Thom.* 43 and 45:4; *Thom.* 47:3–5; *Thom.* 65–66; and *Thom.* 91:2 and 93–94. See also regarding *Thom.* 16:3 (cf. Luke 12:52–53), James M. Robinson, in *Q 12:49–59: Children against Parents — Judging the Time — Settling Out of Court*, Documenta Q: Reconstructions of Q through Two Centuries of Gospel Research Excerpted, Sorted, and Evaluated (Leuven: Peeters, 1997), 119–21.

36. James M. Robinson and Christoph Heil, "Zeugnisse eines schriftlichen, griechischen vorkanonischen Textes: Mt 6,28b ℵ*, P.Oxy. 655 I,1–17 (EvTh 36) und Q 12,27," *Zeitschrift für die neutestamentliche Wissenschaft* 89 (1998): 30–44. See also Robinson's forthcoming essays, "A Written Greek Sayings Cluster Older Than Q: A Vestige," *Harvard Theological Review* 92 (1999), and "The Pre-Q Text of the (Ravens and) Lilies: Q 12:22–31 and P. Oxy. 655 (Gos. Thom. 36)," *Text und Geschichte: Facetten historisch-theologischen Arbeitens aus dem Freundes- und Schülerkreis. Dieter Lührmann zum 60. Geburtstag* (Marburger Theologische Studien, 1999).

back and forth between the *Thomas* and synoptic traditions no doubt occurred, leaving its mark probably on both traditions. However, this is different from supposing that *Thomas* was generated out of the synoptic texts through wholesale borrowing of material. In my opinion, the evidence does not support this view.[37]

Finally, there was the assumption that the Gnostic ideas we find in *Thomas* belong to the second century, where, it was believed, Gnosticism originated as a Christian heresy. This view is also outmoded today, due in large measure to the discovery at Nag Hammadi itself. We now know that Gnosticism was not simply a Christian heresy of the second century. Among the Nag Hammadi texts are several examples of non-Christian Gnosticism, especially of the Sethian school of thought, an early form of *Jewish* Gnosticism. One such text, *Eugnostos the Blessed,* has been dated by its introducer in *The Nag Hammadi Library in English* to the first century B.C.E.[38] Whether this early dating for *Eugnostos* will ultimately prevail in the discussion (it is currently

---

37. This was the conclusion I drew in part one of *Gospel of Thomas and Jesus,* 9–110. Most scholars working on *Thomas* today share this view. However, this does not preclude other creative solutions that might better account for the sometimes puzzling evidence that confronts us in *Thomas* at every turn. Recently, Hans-Martin Schenke ("Compositional History") has pointed to a number of narrative spurs in *Thomas* that suggest to him that many of these sayings may have been extracted from a narrative gospel, though not any of the narrative gospels known to us today. Risto Uro has argued that the *Gospel of Thomas* may have been influenced by the synoptic gospels indirectly in a process he calls "secondary orality," wherein the oral tradition would have been influenced by the synoptic texts, and then in turn influenced the text of *Thomas* (" 'Secondary Orality' in the Gospel of Thomas: Logion 14 as a Test Case," *Forum* 9 nos. 3/4 [1993]: 305–29). His views are similar to those of Klyne Snodgrass, "The Gospel of Thomas: A Secondary Gospel," *Second Century* 7 (1989–90): 19–38.

38. For a description of Sethian Gnosticism see H.-M. Schenke, "The Phenomenon and Significance of Gnostic Sethianism," in B. Layton, ed., *The Rediscovery of Gnosticism: Proceedings of the Conference at Yale, March 1978* (Leiden: Brill, 1981), 2: 588–616. For the dating of *Eugnostos the Blessed* see Douglas M. Parrott's introduction in J. M. Robinson,

unchallenged) remains to be seen. However, it is clear that one cannot assume today, as many did a generation ago, that Gnostic ideas belong exclusively in the heretical Christian sects of the second century and later. Gnostic ideas certainly existed in the first century and would have influenced Christianity as they did other religious traditions. *Thomas* may be our best evidence for the early stages of Gnostic influence among Christians.

It now seems most likely that with the *Gospel of Thomas* we do indeed have a new text, whose traditions are for the most part not derivative of other, better-known gospels, and which was originally written at a time more or less contemporaneous with the canonical gospel texts. What will the new information gleaned from this text tell us about early Christianity? What more can be said about *Thomas* Christianity itself? And how will the *Gospel of Thomas* help us to understand better the texts and communities of early Christianity about which we already know much but would like to know more? This work is only just now beginning, but it is already challenging some old canons in New Testament scholarship. For example, it was once thought that Pauline Christianity formed a clean break with groups influenced more by the words and deeds of Jesus. *Thomas* muddies the waters of this once clear situation. We have already seen how the *Thomas* tradition of understanding Jesus in terms of speculative Jewish wisdom theology and Gnosticism might help us better understand the Christianity that took root in Paul's Corinth (see above, pp. 49–51). But *Thomas* may also help us better understand Paul himself.[39] For example, it was once thought that the inclusion of Gentiles without the necessity of being circumcised was advocated primarily (if not exclusively) within Pauline Christianity. But now we can see that the Pauline churches were not alone in this position:

---

ed., *The Nag Hammadi Library in English* (1988, 1990, 1996, see below), 221.

39. See Patterson, "Paul and the Jesus Tradition," 31–35.

¹His disciples said to him: "Is circumcision beneficial, or not?"

²He said to them: "If it were beneficial, their father would beget them circumcised from their mother. ³But the true circumcision in the spirit has prevailed over everything."   (*Thom.* 53)

The *Gospel of Thomas* may have a similar effect on Johannine studies. Scholars have generally taken the very different content and theology of the Gospel of John as indicative of its relative autonomy with respect to the synoptic Jesus tradition. The synoptic gospels stand in one thought world, a world grounded in the words and deeds of Jesus, while John stands in another, more speculative thought world related to Gnosticism and Hellenistic Judaism. For this reason John has generally been considered rather exotic and more distant from Jesus and Christian origins than the synoptic tradition. But *Thomas* disturbs this tranquil scene as well. Here is a gospel whose theology is quite similar to that which we find in John, and yet it presents this theology using the sayings of Jesus, many of which are paralleled in the synoptic gospels. Thus, *Thomas* demonstrates the potential for the tradition of Jesus' sayings to develop in ways that were once quite unexpected. But once we have seen this potential in the *Thomas* tradition, it becomes easier to see signs of it also in John, signs that might have been overlooked before. We have already seen, for example, echoes of *Thomas* in John 8:51: "Truly I say to you, whoever keeps my word will never taste death," or John 6:68, where Peter proclaims, "You [Jesus] have the words of eternal life." Such sayings seem out of place in John, for here Jesus very seldom utters a saying one might "keep." Rather, John's Jesus seems always to be talking about himself, not offering insight about life or how it ought to be lived. Such sayings must have originated in a literary and theological milieu much more akin to what we find in *Thomas* (see *Thom.* Introduction, Saying 1). Was there perhaps an early, as yet undetected stage in the Johannine tradition when more focus was placed on sayings of

Jesus? Might John have even known the *Thomas* tradition?[40] These are questions that we are only just now in a position to begin posing anew.

9. The *Gospel of Thomas* and the Historical Jesus

One of the reasons the *Gospel of Thomas* was such an exciting find was that its sayings are attributed to *Jesus*. The first question on everyone's mind when the new gospel appeared was whether and to what extent it might give us new information about Jesus of Nazareth. Before this question could be answered responsibly, however, it was necessary first to understand the new gospel on its own terms. Like the other gospels, *Thomas* is not first and foremost a source for information about Jesus. It is an interpretation of Jesus. Once that interpretive voice is understood, it might then be possible to hear in it the remains of that earlier voice it aims to interpret. Now, after fifty years, the state of *Thomas* research is such that this gospel can be integrated into the discussion of the historical Jesus.

There are three ways in which *Thomas* has begun to make an impact on the quest for the historical Jesus: by providing new sayings to be considered as sayings of Jesus; by offering independent versions of sayings already known from the tradition, so that their history and development can now be understood better; and by adding another perspective from which to view the overall development of the Jesus tradition, and so better to understand its origins.

The first area is perhaps the least significant. From the several attempts to find new sayings of Jesus in the *Gospel of Thomas* the results have been meager. Joachim Jeremias

---

40. Cf. Helmut Koester's remarks in "Gnostic Sayings and Controversy Traditions in John 8:12–59," in C. W. Hedrick and R. Hodgson Jr., eds., *Nag Hammadi, Gnosticism, and Early Christianity* (Peabody, Mass.: Hendrickson, 1986), 97–110. That John might have known the *Thomas* tradition and reacted against it is the view expressed by Gregory Riley in *Resurrection Reconsidered*.

thought that *Thom.* 82 and 98 might be authentic sayings of Jesus.[41] Johannes Bauer added *Thom.* 81, 58, 51, and 52 to this list.[42] R. McL. Wilson considered *Thom.* 39, 102, and 47 as possible candidates.[43] The Jesus Seminar voted no new sayings in *Thomas* into the "red" category (= authentic), but did consider *Thom.* 97, the parable of the broken jar, "pink" (= probably authentic).[44] If one had thought that *Thomas* would add many new sayings to the corpus of things Jesus said, these results are disappointing. But that does not mean that the *Gospel of Thomas* has not played an important role in the latest phase of the Jesus debate.

Much more important has been the way in which the *Gospel of Thomas* has contributed to a better understanding of the tradition history of those sayings for which there are versions in both *Thomas* and the synoptic gospels. Where *Thomas* is truly an independent source for these sayings, it can give us critical leverage for seeing how they developed in the course of their transmission in various settings of the early church. By comparing two independent versions of a single saying, one can easily identify those shared aspects as belonging to an early, common version of it — perhaps even the original — while those elements that are unique to one version or the other should more likely be seen as later and not original. Sometimes this procedure has produced some rather striking results. For example, many years ago the parables scholar C. H. Dodd proposed an early version of Mark's parable of the wicked tenants (Mark 12:1–11) that lacked the allegorical features that link the parable so well to Mark's story of Jesus. But without an independent version of the parable against which to compare it, Dodd's

41. J. Jeremias, *The Parables of Jesus,* 2d rev. ed. (New York: Charles Scribner's Sons, 1972), 196–97.

42. J. Bauer, "Echte Jesusworte," in W. C. van Unnik, *Evangelien aus dem Nilsand* (Frankfurt: Heinrich Scheffer, 1960), 124–30.

43. R. McL. Wilson, *Studies in the Gospel of Thomas* (London: A. R. Mowbray, 1960), 75–78.

44. R. W. Funk, B. B. Scott, and J. R. Butts, *The Parables of Jesus: Red Letter Edition* (Sonoma, Calif.: Polebridge, 1988), 61.

reconstruction remained pure speculation. With the discovery of *Thomas*, however, Dodd's skills as a form critic were confirmed: here was a version of the parable (*Thom.* 65) in exactly the form Dodd said it should be.[45]

It is not always the case that *Thomas* offers a more original version of a saying or parable. The *Thomas* tradition also comes with its interpretive tendencies over against which the synoptic version must serve as a control. The point is that with the *Gospel of Thomas* we now have a second source to be used together with the synoptic tradition to arrive at a more original version of the sayings they hold in common.[46] This means, however, that for the first time a noncanonical source has been brought in to address a question that should have profound implications for Christian theology: what did Jesus actually say? Not everyone is comfortable with allowing a text considered by many to be heretical into that exclusive club. But historical honesty and integrity of method have made it difficult to keep the *Gospel of Thomas* out of the discussion, and unmasked some lingering prejudice in an area of research that strives for scholarly fairness.

The *Gospel of Thomas* has helped us to understand better the development of certain individual sayings, but what about the tradition as a whole? When one strings together all of these smaller findings, do any patterns emerge? This

---

45. As noted by B. B. Scott, *Hear, Then, the Parable* (Minneapolis: Fortress, 1989), 237–38.

46. The most thorough attempt to assess the transmission history of the sayings of Jesus taking *Thomas* into account is that of John Dominic Crossan, *In Fragments: The Aphorisms of Jesus* (San Francisco: Harper & Row, 1983). Crossan has also worked to integrate *Thomas* into the discussion of Jesus' parables; see his *In Parables: The Challenge of the Historical Jesus* (New York: Harper & Row, 1973). More recently, one may also see the influence of *Thomas* in several major works on parables: B. B. Scott, *Hear, Then, the Parable;* James Breech, *The Silence of Jesus* (Philadelphia: Fortress, 1983); and Charles Hedrick, *Jesus' Parables as Poetic Fictions: The Creative Voice of Jesus* (Peabody, Mass.: Hendrickson, 1994). The pioneer in this work, however, was Joachim Jeremias, who had begun to integrate *Thomas*'s parables into revised editions of his *Parables of Jesus* already in 1962.

is the third way in which *Thomas* has come to affect the recent Jesus debate. When one compares the sayings of Jesus in *Thomas* with their synoptic counterparts, two things stand out as distinctive of the synoptic side of the tradition: concern with Jesus' suffering and death; and the assumption of an apocalyptic world view. The second of these in particular has proven to be quite important in the most recent phase of research into the historical Jesus. For almost a century, most scholars have held the view that Jesus was an apocalyptic prophet who believed that the world as he knew it was about to come to a end. This view, of course, comes from the synoptic gospels, in which Jesus appears as just such a figure. That he is not such an apocalyptic figure in the Gospel of John was chalked up to John's eccentricity and distance from the more original synoptic tradition. Then the *Gospel of Thomas* appeared, with its dozens of parallels to the synoptic gospels, but without their characteristic apocalyptic slant. In addition to showing the potential of the Jesus tradition to move in ways not previously anticipated, this absence of apocalyptic in *Thomas* raised the question of whether Jesus himself may have lacked this apocalyptic view of the world after all. Perhaps it was just this shift away from apocalyptic that separated Jesus from John the Baptist. Could it be that Jesus was not an apocalyptic prophet, as so many have imagined him since Albert Schweitzer presented him thus almost a century ago?[47] These new discussions take

---

47. Albert Schweitzer, *The Quest of the Historical Jesus,* trans. W. Montgomery, in more recent editions with an Introduction by James M. Robinson (New York: Macmillan, 1968; German original published in 1906). A nonapocalyptic understanding of Jesus has been advocated especially by John Dominic Crossan, *The Historical Jesus: The Life of a Mediterranean Jewish Peasant* (San Francisco: HarperSanFrancisco, 1991). Marcus Borg (*Jesus: A New Vision* [San Francisco: Harper & Row, 1987]) shares this view, but is not so influenced by *Thomas* in arriving at it. This view of Jesus is also widely shared by scholars who have participated in the Jesus Seminar and the Historical Jesus Section of the Society of Biblical Literature (see Borg's polling of these two groups in "A Temperate Case for a Non-Eschatological Jesus," *Forum* 2/3 [1986]: 98–99). For an account of how Borg, Crossan, and others have

in more than just the *Gospel of Thomas,* but *Thomas* has played a significant role in calling into question the synoptic view of Jesus as necessarily historical, and opened up new possibilities for seeing him in different ways.

After fifty years the study of the *Gospel of Thomas* has made great strides.[48] But there is still much that we do not understand about *Thomas* and *Thomas* Christianity. And there is still much to be said about the full significance of *Thomas* for our understanding of Christian origins, and even Jesus himself. But as we publish this volume it seems that interest in this fascinating text continues to grow, especially among younger scholars. It is hoped that presenting the work of the Berlin Working Group for Coptic Gnostic Studies in this format will serve to encourage and advance this research, and thus contribute to the coming of age of this ancient gospel in modern scholarship.

---

come to this conclusion, see Stephen J. Patterson, "The End of Apocalypse: Rethinking the Eschatological Jesus," *Theology Today* 52 (1995): 29–48.

48. For a review of the scholarship done on *Thomas* to date see the surveys of F. T. Fallon and R. Cameron, "The Gospel of Thomas: A Forschungsbericht and Analysis," in W. Haase and H. Temporini, eds., *Aufstieg und Niedergang der römischen Welt* 2/25, no. 6 (Berlin and New York: de Gruyter, 1988), 4213–24, and G. J. Riley, "The *Gospel of Thomas* in Recent Scholarship," *Currents in Research: Biblical Studies* 2 (Sheffield: Sheffield Academic Press, 1994), 227–52. For a thoughtful consideration of future prospects for research, see Philip Sellew, "The Gospel of Thomas: Prospects for Future Research," in John D. Turner and Anne McQuire, eds., *The Nag Hammadi Library after Fifty Years: Proceedings of the 1995 Society of Biblical Literature Commemoration,* Nag Hammadi and Manichaean Studies 44 (Leiden: Brill, 1997), 327–46.

Nag Hammadi: The First Fifty Years*

JAMES M. ROBINSON

I propose here to discuss the significance of the discovery of the Nag Hammadi codices fifty years ago, in terms of what they have meant for the discipline of New Testament scholarship. This significance is not limited to such specific issues as Gnosticism and the New Testament. My focus here is rather in terms of the sociology of knowledge: what has this important manuscript discovery, and the way it was handled over the past half-century, effected in the shaping of biblical studies as a discipline?

1. The Discovery of the Nag Hammadi Library

The Nag Hammadi codices were discovered toward the end of 1945. But how this date came to be established is some-

---

*An abridgement of a plenary address given 19 November 1995 at the annual meeting of the Society of Biblical Literature on the occasion of the fiftieth anniversary of the Nag Hammadi discovery. It was published in *The Nag Hammadi Library after Fifty Years: Proceedings of the 1995 Society of Biblical Literature Commemoration,* ed. John D. Turner and Anne McGuire, Nag Hammadi and Manichaean Studies 44 (Leiden, New York, Cologne: Brill, 1997), 3–33. An earlier draft of this lecture was given at the Institute for Antiquity and Christianity on 21 September 1995.

thing of a saga in its own right, and so can be narrated in
some detail just to give a feel for the region, the participants,
and how the discovery actually took place.

A young French graduate student and adventurer, Jean
Doresse, originally the only source of information about the
discovery, had dated it variously and without explanation
to the beginning of 1946,[1] then more generally 1946,[2] then
1945,[3] then 1947[4] or even 1948.[5] Hence I sought to find
more precise information about the time, place, participants,
and specifics of the discovery.

The most obvious place to begin had apparently never
been consulted: the Acquisitions Registry of the Coptic Museum in Cairo. Here the name of the person who sold the
first codex, Codex III, to the Coptic Museum on 4 October 1946 for £E 250 is listed by name: Rāghib Andarāwus
"al-Qiss" 'Abd al-Sayyid. I tracked him down in retirement
in September of 1975 in the town of Qinā in upper Egypt,
and he gave me information making it possible to unravel
the whole story, with the help of the discoverer himself,

---

1. Henri-Charles Puech and Jean Doresse, "Nouveaux écrits gnostiques découverts en Egypte," in Académie des Inscriptions et Belles-
Lettres *Comptes Rendus des Séances de l'Année 1948* (1948): 89.

2. "It was about 1946." J. Doresse, "Une bibliothèque gnostique
copte," *La Nouvelle Clio* 2 (1949): 61.

3. "Toward 1945." J. Doresse, "Sur les traces des papyrus gnostiques:
Recherches à Chénoboskion," in Académie royale de Belgique *Bulletin de
la Classe des Lettres et des Sciences morales et politiques*, 5th ser. vol. 36
(1950): 433; see also *Les livres secrets des gnostiques d'Egypte*, vol. 1,
Introduction aux écrits gnostiques coptes découverts à Chénoboskion
(Paris: Librairie Plon, 1958), 145; vol. 2 *L'Evangile selon Thomas ou les
paroles secrètes de Jésus* (Paris: Librairie Plon, 1959), 1; "Les gnostiques
d'Egypte," *La Table Ronde* 107 (1956): 86.

4. J. Doresse, "Une importante découverte: Un papyrus gnostique
copte du IVème siècle," *La Bourse Egyptienne*, 10 January 1948, reprinted
in *Chronique d'Egypte* 23 (1948): 260. This dating is erroneously based
on the date of the acquisition of Codex III by the Coptic Museum, not the
discovery itself.

5. From an interview with Doresse by Georges Fradier, *UNESCO Features* 2 (1 August 1949): 11: "It was a year ago, on the shore of the
Nile...."

Muḥammad ʿAlī al-Sammān, in the hamlet al-Qaṣr across the Nile from Nag Hammadi.

Muḥammad ʿAlī, a rustic peasant, was not able to put a calendar date to the discovery so many years after the fact. But it was associated in his mind with two things much more important to him at the time: when the local sugarcane harvest was over and the land lay fallow during the brief winter, he regularly dug at the foot of the cliff soft earth that served as fertilizer for the fields. He had been digging fertilizer, he recalled, just a few weeks before the Coptic Christmas, which occurs on 6 January, when he made the discovery. This suggests that the discovery was in a December.

With regard to the year, he again could speak of it only in terms more important to him at the time: the murder of his father in a blood feud. Muḥammad ʿAlī's memory of that tragedy was as follows: One night his father, a night watchman for valuable irrigation machinery that had been imported from Germany, killed a marauder from the nearby village Ḥamra Dūm, a village that had an ongoing blood feud with Muḥammad ʿAlī's own village al-Qaṣr. On the next day, that murder was avenged when Muḥammad ʿAlī's father was himself found shot through the head, lying where he had only twenty-four hours earlier killed the man from Ḥamra Dūm. Muḥammad ʿAlī's mother, beside herself, told her seven sons to keep their mattocks sharp so as to be ready when an occasion for revenge presented itself.

Muḥammad ʿAlī regretted that he had had to wait some half a year before the opportunity came to avenge his father's death by murdering the man who did it. His memory of revenge was as follows: Someone ran to his house to tell the family that the murderer, Aḥmad Ismāʿīl, was asleep in the heat of the day on a dirt road nearby, with a jug of sugarcane molasses, the local product, by his side. The sons grabbed their mattocks, fell on the hapless person before he could flee, hacked him up, cut open his heart, and, dividing it among them, ate it raw — the ultimate act of blood vengeance.

But this new victim was from Ḥamra Dūm, the opposing village in a longstanding blood feud with al-Qaṣr. Since Ḥamra Dūm lay just at the foot of the cliff on whose talus the discovery had been made, it claimed that area as its turf. Hence, Muḥammad ʿAlī's act of vengeance meant that he no longer dared return to the area of the discovery, which had taken place about a month before he avenged his father's death. So if the date of the father's death could be established, then the date of the discovery itself, about half a year later, could be calculated.

The Nag Hammadi real estate taxation office maintains a registry of deaths. A Copt I knew worked there and was able to locate the entry, giving the cause of death as "unknown" and the date in 1945 as 7 May. If the vengeance was some half a year later, about a month after the discovery, the discovery itself had to have been in November or December of 1945.

The story of the blood feud had come out in connection with Muḥammad ʿAlī explaining why he would not accompany me to the cliff to show me the site of the discovery. So I had to go to Ḥamra Dūm myself, find the son of Aḥmad Ismāʿīl, the man Muḥammad ʿAlī had butchered, and get his assurance that, since he had long since shot up a funeral cortège of Muḥammad ʿAlī's family, wounding Muḥammad ʿAlī and killing a number of his clan, he considered the score settled. Hence, he would not feel honor-bound to attack Muḥammad ʿAlī if he returned to the foot of the cliff. I took this good news back to Muḥammad ʿAlī, who opened his shirt, showed me the scar on his chest, bragged that he had been shot but not killed, yet emphasized that if he ever laid eyes on Aḥmad Ismāʿīl again, he would kill him on the spot. As a result of this display of a braggadocio's fearlessness, he could be persuaded to go to the cliff, camouflaged in my clothes, in a government jeep, with me sitting on the "bullets" side facing the village and him on the safer cliff side, at dusk in Ramadan, when all Muslims are at home eating their fill after fasting throughout the daylight hours.

Of course, this was only the beginning of the story of the

discovery. The codices had now to move from the foot of the cliff into the hands of the Egyptian authorities. But this was no simple matter. It happened as follows:[6] Muḥammad 'Alī had at first feared to open the jar (sealed with a bowl attached with bitumin in the mouth of the jar), lest it contain a jinn. But then it occurred to him that it might contain gold. This gave him courage enough to break it with his mattock. Out flew, up into the air, what he thought might be an airy golden jinn, but I suspect was merely papyrus fragments. He was very let down to find only worthless old books in the jar.

He tore up some of the books to divide them among the other camel drivers who were present, which explains some of the damage and loss that does not fit the pattern of what one would expect from the gradual deterioration over the centuries. Since the other camel drivers, no doubt out of fear of Muḥammad 'Alī, declined his insincere offer to share, he stacked it all back up together, unrolled the turban from around his head, put the codices in it, slung it over his shoulder, unhobbled his camel, drove back home, and dumped the junk in the enclosed courtyard of his house where the animals and their fodder were kept. His mother confirmed to

---

6. For more detailed presentations see my "Introduction" in James M. Robinson and Marvin W. Meyer, eds., *The Nag Hammadi Library in English* (1988, 1990, 1996, see below); "The Discovery of the Nag Hammadi Codices," *Biblical Archaeologist* 42 (fall 1979): 206–24, unabridged with footnotes as "From the Cliff to Cairo: The Story of the Discoverers and the Middlemen of the Nag Hammadi Codices," in *Colloque international sur les textes de Nag Hammadi (Québec, 22–25 août 1978)*, Bibliothèque copte de Nag Hammadi, ed. B. Barc, Section "Etudes" 1 (Québec: Les presses de l'Université Laval, 1981 [1982]), 21–58; "The Discovering and Marketing of Coptic Manuscripts: The Nag Hammadi Codices and the Bodmer Papyri," in *Sundries in Honour of Torgny Säve-Söderbergh*, Acta Universitatis Uppsaliensis, *Boreas: Uppsala Studies in Ancient Mediterranean and Near Eastern Civilizations* 13 (1984): 97–114, reprinted in *The Roots of Egyptian Christianity*, Studies in Antiquity and Christianity, ed. B. A. Pearson and J. E. Goehring (Philadelphia: Fortress, 1986), 1–25.

me that she had in fact burnt some of it along with straw as kindling in the outdoor clay oven.

The family first tried to sell the books for an Egyptian pound or so, but no one offered to buy them. Some were bartered for cigarettes or oranges. A Copt told Muḥammad ʿAlī that they were books of the church, which probably meant only that the Copt recognized the Coptic alphabet enough to know they were not written in Arabic but in Coptic. Since the police were repeatedly searching Muḥammad ʿAlī's home for incriminating evidence of the blood-vengeance murder, he deposited one book — Codex III — with a Coptic priest, knowing that his house would not be searched. For the British had made it clear to the Muslim police that they were not to give the Copts too hard a time, for fear of inciting incidents between Copts and Muslims.

The priest gave this codex to his brother-in-law, a circuit-riding teacher of history and English in the parochial Coptic schools (the only schools in the region prior to President Nasser), who once a week stayed overnight at the priest's home the day he taught at al-Qaṣr. This parochial school teacher was Rāghib Andarāwus "al-Qiss" ʿAbd al-Sayyid. Recall that it was his name I had originally found at the Coptic Museum in Cairo, listed there as the seller of Codex III! At the end of the summer of 1946, he had taken Codex III to Cairo to sell. But when he showed it to an educated Copt, Georgy "Bei" Sobhy, to learn its value, he was, much to his horror, turned in to the authorities. He felt lucky to be permitted finally to sell his book to the Coptic museum (for £E 300, from which a "gift" to the Museum of £E 50 was deducted) and return home without being put in prison.

One of the leading Cairo antiquities dealers at the time, the Cypriot Phocion J. Tano(s), was alerted by peasants from al-Qaṣr working at Giza near Cairo that there had been a manuscript discovery near their hometown. He alerted a provincial dealer of Qinā, with whom he had ongoing business dealings, Zakī Basṭā, to investigate, who in turn alerted his agent in al-Qaṣr, Bahīj ʿAlī, notorious there as a one-eyed outlaw. Bahīj ʿAlī did in fact get two codices for a pittance and, accompanied by Zakī Basṭā, took them to Cairo to sell. Prof. Jacques Schwartz of the University of Strasbourg has narrated how he, as a graduate student at the Institut français d'archéologie orientale in Cairo, had received a phone call from the M. A. Mansour antique shop at Shepherds Hotel to come and see some manuscripts, whose description makes it possible to identify them as Codices II and VII. His report about his visit agrees with that of Zakī Basṭā, who observed from the back of the shop the two "foreigners" (Schwartz, accompanied by Charles Kuentz, director of the French Institute), who came to look at the books but did not buy. Hence Zakī Basṭā and Bahīj ʿAlī sold them to Tano.

On returning to al-Qaṣr, Bahīj ʿAlī promptly acquired all that was left in the possession of Muḥammad ʿAlī's family and sold them in Cairo to Tano. But this time he went alone, since, as he explained, he now knew the way, that is to say, he left out Zakī Basṭā, who commented bitterly that Bahīj ʿAlī did not want this time to have to divide the profit. Instead, Bahīj ʿAlī, with the undivided profits from the sale, was able to buy a farm, a flagrant show of wealth for which Muḥammad ʿAlī never forgave him.

Most of the codices were thus acquired ultimately by Tano, who was pressured into entrusting them for safe-keeping to the governmental department of antiquities. But the shift from King Farouk to President Nasser meant that they were ultimately nationalized and deposited in the Coptic Museum. The long drawn-out but ultimately unsuccessful legal proceedings that Tano undertook to repossess them made the bulk of the codices inaccessible throughout the first half of the 1950s.

2. The Monopolizing of the Nag Hammadi Codices

The first plans to publish materials from the Nag Hammadi codices were undertaken by French scholars. It so happened that the director of the Coptic Museum, Togo Mina, had been a classmate in Paris of Jean and Marianne Doresse, and in fact had proposed (unsuccessfully) to Marianne before she married Jean. He welcomed them to the Coptic Museum on their first visit to Cairo in the fall of 1947, proudly showed them Codex III, and offered to copublish it with Doresse (though Mina had also shown it on 5 December 1946 to François Daumas, and offered to copublish it with him). Mina also took Doresse to an antique shop in Cairo owned by Albert Eid to see some forty leaves of a similar codex — Codex I — which was later smuggled out of Egypt and taken as far as Ann Arbor, Michigan in an effort to sell it. Finally it was bought by the Jung Institute in Zürich for $8,000 contributed by an American expatriate, George H. (Tony) Page, and hence is known as the Jung Codex.[7]

When the French-educated director of the Coptic Museum, Togo Mina, died prematurely in 1949, he was succeeded by the German-educated Pahor Labib. Then the Egyptian revolution in 1952 led to the expulsion of the French director of the *Services des Antiquités,* Abbé Etienne Drioton, under whom Mina had studied in Paris. Finally, the Suez crisis of 1956 resulted in a complete break in diplomatic relations between France and Egypt. All that the French had left to show for their efforts was an international committee dominated by Doresse's professor Henri-Charles Puech (who by now had cut Doresse himself out of the committee, no doubt as academically unqualified and no longer needed). The committee had been convened in Cairo just before the Suez crisis, but achieved no more than to award publication rights for the *Gospel of Thomas* to itself. Official minutes of that meeting were never made available to the committee members, and hence no publication rights were ever actually documented. The committee was never reconvened.

When Coptologists from former East Germany, not com-

---

7. For the details, see my review article, "The Jung Codex: The Rise and Fall of a Monopoly," *Religious Studies Review* 3 (1977): 17–30.

promised in the Suez crisis, began to visit Cairo in 1958, they were welcomed by the new director of the Coptic Museum, Pahor Labib, who awarded them choice publication rights. They then defected to West Germany! Martin Krause and Pahor Labib published the three copies of the *Apocryphon of John* in 1963,[8] while Alexander Böhlig and Labib published *On the Origin of the World* in 1962[9] and the four apocalypses of Codex V in 1963.[10] Their colleagues still in East Germany, Hans-Martin Schenke and Peter Nagel, and of course all other Coptologists from other countries, including the original French team, were cut out of publication rights.[11]

Meanwhile the French counterattacked. In 1961 they enlisted Paris-based UNESCO (United Nations Educational, Scientific, and Cultural Organization) to internationalize the project. At the suggestion of its scholarly advisors, who were of course French, UNESCO officials proposed to photograph all the material, bring it to Paris (which, after all, was where UNESCO was located), and convene in 1962 an international committee to publish it by the end of 1964. But it soon became clear that the Coptic Museum, with Krause's

---

8. *Die drei Versionen des Apokryphon des Johannes im Koptischen Museum zu Alt-Kairo,* Abhandlungen des Deutschen Archäologischen Instituts Kairo, Koptische Reihe 1 (Wiesbaden: Harrassowitz, 1962 [1963]).

9. *Die koptisch-gnostische Schrift ohne Titel aus dem Codex II von Nag Hammadi im Koptischen Museum zu Alt-Kairo,* Deutsche Akademie der Wissenschaften zu Berlin, Institut für Orientforschung 58 (Berlin: Akademie-Verlag, 1962).

10. *Koptisch-gnostische Apokalypsen aus Codex V von Nag Hammadi im Koptischen Museum zu Alt-Kairo, Sonderband* of the *Wissenschaftliche Zeitschrift der Martin-Luther-Universität* (Halle-Wittenberg: Martin-Luther Universität, 1963).

11. A poignant anecdote illustrates the oddity and injustice of the situation: The greatest living Coptologist of the time, Hans Jakob Polotsky, originally of Berlin, but by then of Jerusalem, expressed his amazement that, after his European colleagues had consistently denied him access to the new discovery, the texts should suddenly be offered to him by students from an unknown Institute for Antiquity and Christianity in California, of all places, who had come to Ann Arbor to study Coptic with him at a summer school in 1967.

help, had already assigned the unpublished plums to Krause and Böhlig. For a preliminary committee consisting of Pahor Labib (president), Martin Krause, and Michel Malinine met in Cairo and submitted on 4 November 1961 a report, based on Krause's inventory, proposing that UNESCO be authorized to assign only twenty-three of the forty-eight tractates, on the grounds that the others had already been assigned, were in the press, or had already appeared.

Those listed as already published were I,3[12] (published in 1956); II,1; III,1; IV,1 (actually published, by Krause and Labib, only in 1963); II,2 (published in 1959); II,5 (actually published, by Böhlig and Labib, in 1962); and II,6–7 (actually published, by Krause and Labib, in 1972). Two unedited items were already in the public domain by way of a very modest volume of facsimiles published by Pahor Labib in 1956,[13] and they were listed as assigned to the scholarly world outside of West Germany: II,3 to J. Martin Plumley of England and II,4 to the American Kendrick Grobel (who apparently was never informed of his assignment).

After consultation with Puech and Antoine Guillaumont, the relevant UNESCO official queried: "This seems to me very serious; if a large part of the treatises, and perhaps the richest, are already in the process of publication, is the creation of an International Committee of Publication really justified?" In response to UNESCO's follow-up request for an informed assessment, Guillaumont wrote on 4 December 1961:

> I admit that reading this report causes me some surprise and reveals to me a situation very different from what was presupposed in our previous correspondence rela-

---

12. The standard numeration of Nag Hammadi tractates lists first, in Roman numerals, the number of the codex, then, in Arabic numerals, the number of the tractate in the sequence of that codex.

13. Pahor Labib, *Coptic Gnostic Papyri in the Coptic Museum at Old Cairo*, vol. 1 (Cairo: Government Press, 1956). This is the only volume of this edition to appear.

tive to the Committee envisaged for the publication of the texts of Nag Hammadi....

I note, furthermore, that the treatises presented as already published or to be published by persons already designated are undoubtedly those that have the most interest and that give to the Nag Hammadi discovery its exceptional importance. Only those are left to be distributed by the Committee that offer the least interest and those whose publication, in view of their poor state or their fragmentary condition, will be especially thankless.

Upon the invitation addressed to me last July 4 by the Director General of UNESCO, I agreed quite gladly to become part of a Committee whose stated objective was the publication of the whole of the Nag Hammadi texts; it was, moreover, stated that this Committee would have for its task, at its first meeting, to work out the plan of the publication and to divide the work among the competent specialists. Now it seems to me evident that, in the conditions defined by the report, the Committee is from now on dispossessed of this essential antecedent task, for the major and most important part of the Nag Hammadi texts. If its role must be limited to covering with its authority a work organized without it and accomplished outside of its effective control, I for my part think that it no longer has any *raison d'être*.

UNESCO decided to limit itself to a facsimile edition, whose photography it was willing to fund. The French, now that the West Germans had gotten the remaining plums, lost interest. After all, the French had gotten control of the initial plum they had detected while France still held the monopoly, the *Gospel of Thomas* (II,2), and also had control of the Jung Codex (Codex I) in Zürich. Thus, by the mid-1960s, the Nag Hammadi codices had fallen into the hands of two scholarly cartels, one French and one West German, who monopolized all access to and work on the important new texts.

3. The Breaking of the Monopoly on the Nag Hammadi Codices

During a sabbatical year as Annual Professor at the American School of Oriental Research in Jerusalem in 1965–66, I went to Cairo to find out the status of the Nag Hammadi codices, first in March of 1966, and again in April, on the way to the congress on the origins of Gnosticism at Messina, Sicily. The meager information I was able to obtain in Cairo made me an instant authority on such matters at the congress! So I was appointed to a committee to compose a telegram to UNESCO endorsed by the congress, urging UNESCO to complete the photography, which, by then, was languishing. On passing through Paris shortly thereafter, I inquired if the telegram had been received and acted upon. I was told that the last 314 photographs had indeed arrived in Paris on 6 June 1966. And I was assured that publication would be completed by the end of 1968. I was of course pleased with such good news, but in more cynical retrospect realize that the publication timetable was at best wishful thinking, if not just an effective way to get me out of the office.

The German Archaeological Institute in Cairo had, on my April trip, given me access to Nag Hammadi photographs on file there, and I had worked twenty-four hours a day for a couple of days copying them. Then in June, I passed through Münster, Germany, to give a guest lecture at the university. In the process, I was lent some transcriptions by Martin Krause, which I stayed up all night copying by hand the night before my German lecture. On my return home, I obtained a modest NEH grant for three years, 1967–70, that made it possible to organize a small team to translate these few unpublished tractates, to which I had by such unorthodox means obtained access. We stamped each with a note to the effect that they should not be published, since we had no publication rights to offer. But we did circulate them widely in mimeographed form.

During this three-year grant period, I wrote repeatedly to UNESCO, letters that all went unanswered. The official in charge of the Nag Hammadi matter, N. Bammate, was a member of a gourmet dining club in Paris, but otherwise was quite inactive. When I complained to his superior, I was told that he did not answer letters, since he came from an oral culture (Afghanistan).

I went back to Paris in January of 1968 to ask Bammate personally where things stood; for example, whether the fragments had been identified and placed on the leaves before photography, a prerequisite to using the UNESCO photographs for a facsimile edition that would put the material into the public domain available to all. Rather than bother with shuffling through the photographs to seek to answer my question, he said I could study them myself and write a report to him as to the status of the fragments. He even let me use a UNESCO office empty over the weekend for this purpose. He laid out for me about half of the glossy prints and the negatives of the other half, no doubt so I could not abscond with a complete file.

Saturday morning, I found a photography shop in a Paris suburb willing to work straight through the weekend, and gave them some six hundred negatives to make glossy-print enlargements in time enough for me to pick them and the negatives up by Sunday evening. Meanwhile in the UNESCO office, I laid the glossy prints one by one on the floor under my tripod and clicked away with my simple tourist's camera. Monday morning I turned in to Bammate the negatives and prints that he had lent me.

I also flew to Copenhagen and obtained from Søren Giversen microfilms he had made earlier in Cairo of Codices II, III and IX, which he, however, had not made available to others, on the grounds that Labib did not want the French to get them.

On returning to Claremont, I wrote the desired report and sent it to UNESCO. I now had photographs of all the Nag Hammadi codices.

We enlarged our American Nag Hammadi project membership, ultimately to include some thirty-eight persons. We assigned all the Nag Hammadi tractates, and had produced draft transcriptions and translations of everything by 1970. Then we distributed widely our transcriptions and translations to the Nag Hammadi scholars who had been left out in the cold. This is what in effect broke the monopoly. At the meeting of the Society for New Testament Studies in 1969 in England, I cochaired with R. McL. Wilson a Nag Hammadi seminar, to which I invited Henry Chadwick of Oxford, who had edited the Greek *Sentences of Sextus,* to discuss the Coptic translation in Codex XII that Frederik Wisse had just identified, and Böhlig of Tübingen to analyze the *Paraphrase of Shem* in Codex VII, both on the basis of the transcriptions and translations we had sent them.

We arranged a lecture tour for Böhlig in America, so that he could work with our translators when lecturing on their campuses, and in turn gain access to our material. Böhlig made it possible for Wisse to go to Tübingen and coedit with him the *Gospel of the Egyptians,* for which Böhlig had held the official assignment since 1963. This gave us for the first time some limited publication rights. Such mutually supportive collaboration characterized our procedures from the beginning.

I sent our transcriptions and translations to Kurt Rudolph of Leipzig in East Germany. His report about their contents, which he somewhat naively published in 1969,[14] motivated the head of the French monopoly, Henri-Charles Puech of the Ecole Pratique des Hautes Etudes and the Collège de France, to make a formal protest to UNESCO for having given me access to its photographs. Fortunately UNESCO told him that it was their responsibility to disseminate the cultures of its member states, not to restrict access. So they did not restrict my activity.

---

14. Kurt Rudolph, "Gnosis und Gnostizismus, ein Forschungsbericht," *Theologische Rundschau,* n. F. 34 (1969): 89–120, 181–231, 358–61. The third installment, with the subtitle "Nachträge," consists primarily of corrections I had sent him after reading proofs of the first two installments. He speaks quite openly, for example, p. 359, of "the ongoing work of the editing team in Claremont (USA)" under my leadership.

During the school year 1970–71, I lived in Paris but commuted once a week to Strasbourg as a Fulbright professor at the University of Strasbourg. Each week, I gave a Nag Hammadi colleague, Jacques Ménard, our transcription and translation of a tractate, and the next week discussed it privately with him, while passing on to him another tractate for discussion the following week.

By such means we saw to it that all interested scholars got access to the material. But we still lacked publication rights.

4. The Publishing of All the Nag Hammadi Codices

By 1970 only about a third of the discovery had been published. Only a fifth was available in English translation, no doubt because there had been no English monopoly. The history of a Nag Hammadi scholarship fully open to the whole academic community really began only in 1970.

During my sabbatical year 1970–71 in Paris, I worked in an office lent to me at UNESCO. At my urging, an "International Committee for the Nag Hammadi Codices" was not only nominated by UNESCO and appointed by the Arab Republic of Egypt, but actually convened in Cairo in December of 1970.

Since I had long before arranged with Brill to publish the facsimile edition, Brill had made a plane reservation for their Dutch photographer to fly to Cairo and photograph the material as we restored it, if I could get the committee to accept Brill (rather than some Egyptian firm) as publisher. Amid the pomp and ceremony of the opening day of the Cairo meeting I did arrange to get that much of the agenda acted on and a telegram off to Brill. This timing was crucial, for Brill's plane reservation was for the next day, and, due to the Christmas tourism, there were no plane seats left on later flights.

I proposed that a technical subcommittee stay in Cairo after the formal meeting ended to reassemble the fragmentary leaves, so that a facsimile edition would be possible. I nominated for membership in the technical subcommittee those who had long since had access to the material, and hence had some experience in working at least with photographs: the German delegate Martin Krause, the Swiss delegate Rodolphe Kasser, the Danish delegate Søren Giversen and myself, the American delegate and permanent secretary of the UNESCO committee.

We worked some ten days, and again a fortnight in January, using as our point of departure the mimeographed transcriptions and translations the American team had prepared. Not only each day's results of reassembled leaves, but in fact all the Nag Hammadi materials, were photographed by the Brill photographer, so that complete photographic files came to Leiden and Claremont in 1971. But the job of placing fragments and establishing the sequence of leaves in each codex was far from complete. We returned to Cairo once a year for a week or two as long as UNESCO would pay for the trips. But very many fragments still remained unplaced. I then took two of my students, Charles W. Hedrick and Stephen L. Emmel, for a semester to Cairo in 1974–75, and then left Emmel there for two more years to carry through the last fragment placements until the conservation project was really completed. The Institute for Antiquity and Christianity paid Emmel $100 per month for living expenses in Cairo during that period.

The facsimile edition of the Nag Hammadi codices began publication in the spring of 1972 with the appearance of Codex VI, less than a year and a half after we first got access in Cairo to the papyri themselves. The publication of the last of the thirteen codices, in two volumes of the facsimile edition containing Codex I and Codices IX and X, took place in 1977, in time to be announced in December in a plenary address at the joint annual meeting of the American Academy of Religion and the Society of Biblical Literature in San Francisco.

To meet that deadline, we had an all-too-tight schedule. The last fragment had been placed on 2 September by Emmel in Cairo. This placement got the stamp of approval from our volume editor for the critical edition of the relevant codex, Birger Pearson, on 30 September. Our placement was then phoned through to Frederik Wisse (whom we had, with Böhlig's help, stationed in Tübingen to work closely with the facsimile edition's printing firm in Stuttgart). He added a photo of the new fragment into the photograph of the correct leaf, which was then forwarded to Leiden in time to be bound and hand-carried to the AAR/SBL convention in December by the director of Brill, W. C. Wieder Jr. This meant that eight years after getting access to the originals in Cairo, all thirteen codices had been put into the public domain. Hence we simultaneously published in December of 1977 *The Nag Hammadi Library in English*,[15] our already-prepared English translation. Since then, it has appeared in several editions and sold over a hundred thousand copies.

Meanwhile our fourteen-volume critical edition, with introductions to each tractate, followed by transcripts, translations, notes, and indices, had already begun to appear in 1975 with the *Gospel of the Egyptians* by Alexander Böhlig and Frederik Wisse.[16] The last two volumes, the *Apocryphon of John* by Frederik Wisse and Michael Waldstein,[17] and Codex VII by Birger A. Pearson,[18] appeared 1995.

Our translation team consisted in many cases of the same Americans who went with me to Cairo year after year to

---

15. James M. Robinson and Marvin W. Meyer, eds., *The Nag Hammadi Library in English,* trans. Coptic Gnostic Library Project of the Institute for Antiquity and Christianity (Leiden: Brill, 1977 [pbk. ed. 1984]; San Francisco: Harper & Row, 1977 [pbk. ed. 1981]); 3d rev. ed., ed. James M. Robinson and Richard Smith (San Francisco: Harper & Row; Leiden: Brill, 1988 [HarperCollins pbk. ed. 1990]); reprinted unaltered as 4th rev. ed. (Leiden: Brill, 1996).

16. *Nag Hammadi Codices III,2 and IV,2: The Gospel of the Egyptians (The Holy Book of the Great Invisible Spirit),* ed. and trans. Alexander Böhlig and Frederik Wisse with Pahor Labib, Nag Hammadi Studies (Leiden: Brill, 1975).

17. *The Apocryphon of John: Synopsis of Nag Hammadi Codices II,1; III,1 and IV,1, with Papyrus Berolinensis Gnosticus 8502,2,* ed. Frederik Wisse and Michael Waldstein, Nag Hammadi and Manichaean Studies 33 (Leiden: Brill, 1995).

18. *Nag Hammadi Codex VII,* ed. Birger A. Pearson, Nag Hammadi and Manichaean Studies 30 (Leiden: Brill, 1996 [November 1995]).

place fragments for the facsimile edition and who at the same time were preparing our critical edition. They continue to be prominent in the Nag Hammadi section of SBL created at about that time, and still continuing (now called Nag Hammadi and Gnosticism), currently chaired by John D. Turner. Two have become project directors at the Institute for Antiquity and Christianity, Birger A. Pearson and Marvin W. Meyer, directing projects that grew out of our Nag Hammadi experience. Several are members of the recently reorganized Brill monograph series Nag Hammadi and Manichaean Studies, whose original editorial board had only a small minority of Americans (Hans Jonas, George MacRae, Frederik Wisse, and myself), but whose reorganized board has now a majority (Harold W. Attridge, Ron Cameron, Stephen L. Emmel, Charles W. Hedrick, Howard M. Jackson, Douglas M. Parrott, Birger A. Pearson, and myself). This team has thus matured to give American scholarship an international prominence in Coptology and Gnosticism it never had before.

The copies of our original draft transcriptions and translations given to Jacques Ménard in Strasbourg in 1970–71 became his motivation for organizing at the Université de Laval in Quebec, Canada, the French-Canadian critical edition with commentary, directed by Paul-Hubert Poirier, *La bibliothèque copte de Nag Hammadi*. It began publication in 1977 at Peeters in Leuven and promises to complete its many-volumed edition by the end of the decade.

The Berliner Arbeitskreis für koptisch-gnostische Schriften, led by Hans-Martin Schenke, had obtained on loan the transcriptions and translations I had given to Kurt Rudolph, photographed them, and used this as the source material for their own translation activity. For they had already begun as early as 1958 publishing in the *Theologische Literaturzeitung*[19] translations of the few tractates that were already

---

19. Johannes Leipoldt, "Ein neues Evangelium? Das koptische Thomas-evangelium übersetzt und besprochen," *Theologische Literaturzeitung* 83 (1958): 481–96.

available in the meager volume of facsimiles Pahor Labib had published in Egypt in 1956. With all the material now in hand, their tempo escalated dramatically, and translations were followed by critical editions with commentaries, as dissertations were published. This Berlin group, though now somewhat scattered among the three centers, from Claremont to Quebec and Berlin, is currently working on a complete and definitive German translation to appear in the series Die griechischen christlichen Schriftsteller der ersten Jahrhunderte, as volumes 2 and 3 of the subseries Koptisch-gnostische Schriften.

It is of some cultural-political significance, in terms of the sociology of knowledge, that a manuscript discovery originally monopolized by western Europe — namely, France and West Germany, with Denmark, the Netherlands, and Switzerland playing supporting roles, is no longer dominated by western Europe. Instead, the outsiders, rather than competing among themselves, have banded together to produce the comprehensive and definitive editions: in English, not in England but in America; in French, not in France but in Canada; and in German, not in what was West Germany but in what was East Germany. What used to be considered in this area of research the outer fringes of the western world have thus joined together to become a united, cooperative undertaking. The three teams, representing the three scholarly language areas, have tended to merge into what has become the main strength of Nag Hammadi research in the world today.

5. The New Ethos for Handling Manuscript Discoveries

The publication of the complete facsimile edition, just eight years after first getting access to the papyri themselves, has set an obvious standard for avoiding or overcoming monopolies in other manuscript discoveries. After all, we, though outsiders to the field, had shown that where there is a will there is a way. For the impossibilities ticked off by the insiders usually turned out to be excuses to justify their own self-interest, excuses that could readily be overcome if one really wanted to.

For example: The last bit of the Nag Hammadi monopoly had been the Jung Codex (Codex I), since it was not in Cairo, where we had achieved open access, but in a bank vault in Zürich belonging to the heirs of Carl Gustaf Jung. The heirs were the owners, but had agreed to return the codex to Cairo when the team of editors no longer needed it for their transcription. The spokesman for the editors, Rodolphe Kasser, was on our technical subcommittee, and would still have unlimited access to it in Cairo, had it been returned. But then so could the rest of us! So he maintained that the heirs were not willing to return it because they knew it was worth a lot of money. But then the spokesman for the heirs told me that the Jung family was ready to return it whenever the editors said they no longer needed it in Zürich. He even agreed to write the editors to inquire if he could return it. Thereupon he informed me that all who had responded (a postal strike had prevented the French from responding) had agreed to return it, except...Rodolphe Kasser! Only when Kasser had sent the last volume of their edition to the publisher and thus insured that it would be the *editio princeps* did he agree to the return of the codex to Egypt.[20]

The most obvious comparison to the Nag Hammadi publication experience has been the abysmal publication record of the Dead Sea Scrolls, since both discoveries took place at about the same time and hence have all along been compared in various regards.

At the annual meeting of the Society of Biblical Literature (that year, 1991, in Kansas City, just a week after *A Facsimile Edition of the Dead Sea Scrolls,* which I co-edited had appeared),[21] SBL president Helmut Koester convened a

---

20. See my review article, "The Jung Codex: The Rise and Fall of a Monopoly," *Religious Studies Review* 3 (January 1977): 17–30.

21. Robert H. Eisenman and James M. Robinson, eds., *A Facsim-*

special, called meeting of the society at nine o'clock on the last evening, 25 November. The chair of the research and publications committee read a resolution that had just been officially adopted by SBL:[22]

1. *Recommendation to those who own or control ancient written materials:* Those who own or control ancient written materials should allow all scholars to have access to them. If the condition of the written materials requires that access to them be restricted, arrangements should be made for a facsimile reproduction that will be accessible to all scholars. Although the owners or those in control may choose to authorize one scholar or preferably a team of scholars to prepare an official edition of any given ancient written materials, such authorization should neither preclude access to the written materials by other scholars nor hinder other scholars from publishing their own studies, translations, or editions of the written materials.

2. *Obligations entailed by specially authorized editions:* Scholars who are given special authorization to work on official editions of ancient written materials should cooperate with the owners or those in control of the written materials to ensure publication of the edition in an expeditious manner, and they should facilitate access to the written materials by all scholars. If the owners or those in control grant to specially authorized editors any privileges that are unavailable to other

---

ile Edition of the Dead Sea Scrolls, 2 vols. (Washington, D.C.: Biblical Archaeology Society, 1991; rev. ed. 1992).

22. On 22 November 1991, the research and publications committee had (to quote its minutes) "directed that the statement on access be sent to funding agencies, publishers, primary repositories, be published in *Religious Studies News,* and be circulated through the American Council of Learned Societies to other learned societies interested in literary and artifactual remains (encouraging their participation in policy development). The committee approved further distribution as widely as possible." I had it republished in the *Zeitschrift für Papyrologie und Epigraphik* 92 (1992): 296.

scholars, these privileges should by no means include exclusive access to the written materials or facsimile reproductions of them. Furthermore, the owners or those in control should set a reasonable deadline for completion of the envisioned edition (not more than five years after the special authorization is granted).

When the resolution had been read, Emanuel Tov, then head of the Dead Sea Scrolls project, himself arose and announced that all restrictions on free access to the Dead Sea Scrolls had been officially lifted.[23] You might as well unlock the barn once the horse is stolen.

I hope and trust, and in fact am convinced, that we have all learned a lesson from this sad tale, for which we all bear some collective responsibility, and that in the case of future important manuscript discoveries a much more enlightened policy will be followed.[24] The Nag Hammadi experience deserves some credit for providing positive incentives to such

---

23. As recently as 1 October 1995 Tov had reported by e-mail to the "Judaios: First Century Judaism Discussion Forum," denying rumors that the Israeli authorities had "dropped their objection to the Huntington [Library] action" (which had on 22 September 1991 removed all restrictions on the microfilms of the still unpublished fragments that for years had been stored there by Elizabeth Hay Bechtel, inaccessible to the public), and affirmed that "all of us are still in the middle of deliberations." On 6 October 1991 he wrote the Huntington proposing a meeting to discuss the problem, and requested that the Huntington "delay all access to the scrolls for one month, until the said meeting." The meeting never took place.

24. By pure coincidence I presented an address proposing such policies the same weekend that the Huntington Library made its announcement. It has hence been widely published: *Manuscript Discoveries of the Future*, with an appendix containing the title page, table of contents, introduction, and sample plates from *A Facsimile Edition of the Dead Sea Scrolls*, ed. J. L. Reed, The Institute for Antiquity and Christianity, Occasional Papers 23 (Claremont: IAC, 1991); abridged by James M. Robinson "Avoiding Another Scrolls Access Furor," *Los Angeles Times*, 28 September 1991, sec. F, 13–14; abridged as "Handling Future Manuscript Discoveries," *Biblical Archaeologist* (December 1991): 235–40; abridged by Hershel Shanks, "What We Should Do Next Time Great Manuscripts Are Discovered," *Biblical Archaeology Review* 18, no. 1 (January–February 1992):

a better future, in helping to change the ethos for handling important new manuscript discoveries.[25]

6. The Impact of the Nag Hammadi Discovery on the Shape of New Testament Scholarship

Here it is not my purpose to itemize a series of specific details where the Nag Hammadi texts have influenced the understanding of New Testament texts.[26] Rather my intent is to maintain the focus on the shape of the discipline of biblical scholarship itself as a result of the Nag Hammadi discovery.

The forty-eight Nag Hammadi tractates would have commended themselves to biblical scholarship much more readily if they had been discovered in Palestine or Syria, where many of them were composed, rather than in upper Egypt, where perhaps none of them was composed, and if they had survived not only in late-fourth-century copies of Coptic translations, but also in the original Greek in which the authors wrote in the first three centuries of the Common Era. Hence they caught us academically unprepared. Coptic was at that time only one of the more esoteric dimensions of textual criticism, and had been safely ignored by all the rest of us. It can no longer safely be ignored.

66–70; reprinted in unabridged form in *Zeitschrift für Papyrologie und Epigraphik* 92 (1992): 281–96.

25. In handling the 152 sixth century C.E. charred Greek documentary papyri rolls from the Byzantine church in Petra, a conscious effort seems to have been made to introduce clear new policies: "It will be recalled that all parties involved had signed an access/publication agreement and we are happy to report that the final division of the scrolls for publication purposes between the two groups was agreed to in late 1995" (Pierre M. Bikai, "Update on the Scrolls," *Amman Center of Oriental Research Newsletter* 7, no. 2 [Winter 1995]: 11).

26. Itemized by Hans-Martin Schenke, "The Relevance of Nag Hammadi Research to New Testament Scholarship" (paper presented at the annual meeting of the Society of Biblical Literature, Chicago, Ill., November 1994).

Furthermore our traditional prejudices about Gnosticism had dampened the interest of many. But some of the Nag Hammadi tractates are not Gnostic at all! For example, the *Teachings of Silvanus* (VII,4) is Jewish wisdom literature (somewhat Christianized), and indeed quotes (112,37–113,7) the *Wisdom of Solomon* (7:25–26) as referring to Christ. Thus it involves a secondary Sophia Christology that expands considerably the faint traces in the New Testament itself.

The bulk of the tractates are of course Gnostic, and that has been a stumbling block for many. After all, Gnosticism has commonly been held to be unintelligible, otherworldly, and rather irrelevant mythology, a corruption of earliest Christianity that abandoned the Old Testament and its God — our God — in a Marcion-like perversion. Hence, rather than, with an open mind, seizing upon this library, the first really authentic early Gnostic texts that can speak for themselves, many in our discipline have simply left them to one side. Therefore it is very important to communicate to a wider academic public the surprising results that the specialists have thus far reached, which should lead to a calming of such prejudices.

Rather than being a departure from the Old Testament as the basis of our religious tradition, Gnosticism found there, rather than in Homer or Zoroaster[27] or Gilgamesh, the inspiration for its mythology. The book of Genesis is the favorite authority of Gnosticism! For example, Genesis 3 is retold detail after detail, even if with a typically Gnostic twist, in the *Testimony of Truth* (IX,3). To be sure, the Gnostics did interpret the Old Testament in a different way, as did, however, also Philo, Josephus, the New Testament, Qumran, and Rabbinic Judaism. Hence Gnosticism stands in the biblical tradition as well.

---

27. The tractate *Zostrianos* (VIII,1) concluded with an encoded subscript: "Zostrianos; Oracles of Truth of Zostrianos, God of Truth; Teachings of Zoroaster." The text, however, is not Zoroastrian but Sethian, building on 2 *Enoch*.

In effect, the roots of Gnosticism, previously sought all over the ancient world, have become most visible in Judaism. Even the apocalyptic literature of Judaism itself has been enriched with one Jewish Gnostic apocalypse from Nag Hammadi, the *Apocalypse of Adam* (V,5). George Mac-Rae saw to its inclusion in the current edition of *The Old Testament Pseudepigrapha*.[28] It narrates Adam's deathbed testament to his son Seth, a kind of Gnostic *Heilsgeschichte*, narrating the three descents of the Gnostic redeemer, Seth, to rescue the elect Sethians from flood, fire, and the final cataclysm.

Birger A. Pearson has recently summarized the dependence of Nag Hammadi texts on Jewish apocryphal and pseudepigraphical literature: the *Apocryphon of John* (II,1; III,1; IV,1; Papyrus Berolinensis Gnosticus 8502,2) builds on *1 Enoch;* the *Apocalypse of Adam* (V,5) builds on the *Life of Adam and Eve; Zostrianos* (VIII,1) builds on *2 Enoch*.[29] Here one has before one's very eyes the source material of Gnosticism. All it took was the distinctive Gnostic twist, a powerful push from some kind of alienated Judaism, Samaritanism, or Proselytism, to engender the Gnostic movement and its distinctive literature.

A whole new Jewish sect, to add to the plethora already known to characterize Second Temple Judaism, has come into the clear light of day in the Nag Hammadi codices. Hans-Martin Schenke has brought into focus the Gnostic Sethians, who contributed the largest single cluster to the Nag Hammadi library, eleven of the forty-eight different texts. At the International Conference on the Rediscovery of Gnosticism held at Yale in 1978, one major section of

---

28. James H. Charlesworth, ed., *The Old Testament Pseudepigrapha,* vol. 1, *Apocalyptic Literature and Testaments* (Garden City, N.Y.: Doubleday, 1983), 707–11 (MacRae's introduction), 712–19 (MacRae's translation).

29. Birger A. Pearson, "From Jewish Apocalypticism to Gnosis" (paper presented at the International Conference on the Nag Hammadi Texts in the History of Religions, Copenhagen, Denmark, 19–24 September 1995).

the program and one whole volume of its proceedings were devoted exclusively to Sethianism.[30] The Nag Hammadi Sethian texts can be subdivided into three groups, making it possible to discern roughly the history of Sethianism.[31] Some are only Jewish, with no Christian aspects: the *Three Steles of Seth* (VII,5), the *Thought of Norea* (IX,2), *Marsanes* (X), and *Allogenes* (XI,3); or at most with scant secondarily Christianizing interpolations: the *Apocalypse of Adam* (V,5) and *Zostrianos* (VIII,1). Others have a thin Christian veneer: the *Gospel of the Egyptians* (III,2; IV,2) and the *Trimorphic Protennoia* (XIII,1). Only a minority can be really called Christian Gnosticism: the *Apocryphon of John* (II,1; III,1; IV,1; Papyrus Berolinensis Gnosticus 8502,2), the *Hypostasis of the Archons* (II,4), and *Melchizedek* (IX,1). But this Christian Sethianism is the only kind previously known, having been attested by the heresiologists.[32] The relative rarity of Christian Sethian texts in the Nag Hammadi library is all the more surprising, when one considers that it is, after all, a Christian library, which can of course account for the secondary Christianizing of several of the Jewish Sethian texts. Most of the non-Christian Jewish Sethian texts represent instead a Neoplatonic Gnosticism, as especially John D. Turner has worked out: the *Three Steles of Seth* (VII,5), *Zostrianos* (VIII,1), *Marsanes* (X) and *Al-*

---

30. *The Rediscovery of Gnosticism: Proceedings of the International Conference on Gnosticism at Yale, New Haven, Connecticut, March 28–31, 1978*, vol. 2, *Sethian Gnosticism*, ed. B. Layton, Studies in the History of Religions 41, Supplements to *Numen* (Leiden: Brill, 1981). Itemized by Hans-Martin Schenke, "The Phenomenon and Significance of Gnostic Sethianism," 588–616, and also James M. Robinson, "Sethians and Johannine Thought: The *Trimorphic Protennoia* and the Prologue of the Gospel of John," 643–62, as well as the "Discussion," 662–70, and the "Concluding Discussion," 671–85.

31. See H.-M. Schenke, "Gnosis: Zum Forschungsstand unter besonderer Berücksichtigung der religions-geschichtlichen Problematik, *Verkündigung und Forschung* 32 (1987): 2–21.

32. Irenaeus (*Adversus Haereses* 1.29, "Barbelo-Gnostics"; 1.30, "Ophites" and "Sethians") and Epiphanius (*Panarion* 26, "Gnostics"; 39, "Sethians"; 40, "Archontics."

logenes (XI,3). Thus one can see Sethianism evolving out of Judaism into early Christian and Neoplatonic cultural contexts, much as did mainline Christianity itself. Indeed these history-of-religions trajectories of Sethianism and early Christianity are even more parallel in that both emerged from Jewish baptismal sects.[33]

Nag Hammadi tractates also fill gaps in early Christian trajectories themselves. The first half of the Pauline corpus presents us with authentic letters of Paul, the oldest Christian texts to have survived. Then the second half of the Pauline corpus shows how Paul was variously interpreted after his death. The latest letters in the Pauline corpus, the Pastoral Epistles, display a mild, "safe" Paul that reassured the canonizers to include him after all, in spite of the (mis)use of him being made by Gnostics and Marcionites. Acts tends to confirm this domesticated Paul.

But the earlier Deutero-Pauline Epistles, Colossians and Ephesians, had pointed in a more speculative, cosmic direction. Paul himself had emphasized that the believer is united with Christ, in baptism indeed dying with Christ. But Paul reserved one's resurrection with Christ for the eschatological future, what Ernst Käsemann drew to our attention as Paul's "eschatological reservation."[34] Yet already Col. 2:12 presents the believer as both dying *and* rising with Christ. And Eph. 2:6 affirms God has thereupon enthroned the believer "in heavenly places" with Christ. Is not the believer's resurrection then past already?

The canonical texts hesitate actually to put it that way.

---

33. Jean-Marie Sevrin has worked out the baptismal dimensions of Sethianism in *Le dossier baptismal séthien: Etudes sur la sacramentaire gnostique,* Bibliothèque copte de Nag Hammadi, Section "Etudes" 2 (Québec: Les Presses de l'Université Laval, 1986).

34. Ernst Käsemann, invited to make a presentation at a faith and order conference, asked me to verify the English translation of his essay that had been prepared for him. His key term, "eschatologischer Vorbehalt," came through in English in a completely unintelligible way that would lead the audience inevitably to miss the point. So I coined for him the English formulation "eschatological reservation."

For a Pastoral Epistle condemns the "godless chatter" of Hymenaeus and Philetus, who "will lead people into more and more ungodliness, . . . by holding that the resurrection is past already" (2 Tim. 2:16–18). Here some kind of shadow-boxing is taking place, as the Pastorals allude to some otherwise unattested Christian leaders who clearly had gone too far. The only kind of resurrection for believers that this could be talking about is not physical, but purely spiritual. But if that spiritual resurrection has already taken place, an eschatologically future physical resurrection would have become quite superfluous. Hence the advocates of this "heresy" do not get an unbiased hearing in the New Testament.

But now, the *Treatise on Resurrection* (I,4) presents in a very appealing way precisely this spiritual resurrection that has taken place already, and indeed by appeal to the authority of *the* apostle *par excellence,* Paul! Should not any objective historian trying to trace the Pauline school include this noncanonical epistle as part of the left wing of that school alongside the Pastoral Epistles as documentation for the right wing? Or should we limit our knowledge of the left wing of the Pauline school to the smear by the right wing?[35]

The *Treatise on Resurrection* surely goes further than does Paul himself; indeed it would no doubt have been rejected by Paul, as is indicated by such texts as 1 Cor. 4:8, where "already" is in effect branded as heretical, and Phil. 3:11, 20–21, where the believer's resurrection is clearly still future. But neither are the Pastoral Epistles and Acts written as Paul himself would have written. The fact that we are *their* heirs, rather than heirs of the spiritualized Gnostic option, makes them instinctively more congenial to us. But as critical historians we must analyze all the evidence if we

---

35. See Gerd Lüdemann, *Heretics: The Other Side of Early Christianity* (London: SCM; New York: Westminster/John Knox, 1996), 120–42 for a full presentation of Colossians, Ephesians, the Pastoral Epistles, and the *Treatise on Resurrection* in this regard.

want to assess the full history of the Pauline trajectory or trajectories.

Thus the Nag Hammadi codices have forced us to direct our attention to New Testament "apocrypha" to an extent never before realized. The current edition of Wilhelm Schneemelcher's standard *New Testament Apocrypha* contains eleven Nag Hammadi tractates,[36] and a more recent dictionary article on "New Testament Apocrypha" by Stephen J. Patterson lists thirty-two Nag Hammadi tractates.[37] What is even more significant, Helmut Koester's *Introduction to the New Testament* includes discussions of sixteen Nag Hammadi tractates![38] The field of early Christian Literature has grown immensely, and we must grow with it.

Perhaps the most lively debate going on in New Testament scholarship as a result of the Nag Hammadi discovery has to

---

36. *Neutestamentliche Apokryphen in deutscher Übersetzung*, vol. 1, *Evangelien*, 5th ed., ed. W. Schneemelcher (Tübingen: Mohr/Paul Siebeck, 1990); English trans., *New Testament Apocrypha*, vol. 1, *Gospels and Related Writings*, ed. R. McL. Wilson (Louisville: Westminster/John Knox, 1991): *The Apocryphon of James* (I,2), *The Gospel of Thomas* (II,2), *The Gospel of Philip* (II,3), *The Book of Thomas (the Contender)* (II,7), *The Dialogue of the Savior* (III,5), *The (First) Apocalypse of James* (V,3), *The (Second) Apocalypse of James* (V,4), and *The Letter of Peter to Philip* (VIII,2); vol. 2, *Apostolisches; Apokalypsen und Verwandtes* (1989). English trans. (1992), *Writings Related to the Apostles; Apocalypses and Related Subjects: The Apocalypse of Paul* (V,5), *The Acts of Peter and the Twelve* (VI,1), and *The Apocalypse of Peter* (VII,3).

37. Stephen J. Patterson, "New Testament Apocrypha," *Anchor Bible Dictionary* (New York: Doubleday, 1992), 1.295–96.

38. Helmut Koester, *Introduction to the New Testament*, vol. 2, *History and Literature of Early Christianity* (Philadelphia: Fortress, 1982): *The Apocryphon of James* (I,2), *The Gospel of Truth* (I,3; XII,2), *The Apocryphon of John* (II,1; III,1; IV,1; Papyrus Berolinensis Gnosticus 8502,2), *The Gospel of Thomas* (II,2), *The Hypostasis of the Archons* (II,4), *The Book of Thomas (the Contender)* (II,7), *The Gospel of the Egyptians* (III,2; IV,2), *The Letter of Eugnostos the Blessed* (III,3; V,1), *The Sophia of Jesus Christ* (III,4), *The Dialogue of the Savior* (III,5), *The (First) Apocalypse of James* (V,3), *The (Second) Apocalypse of James* (V,4), *The Apocalypse of Adam* (V,5), *The Paraphrase of Shem* (VII,1), *The Second Treatise of the Great Seth* (VII,2), and the *Three Steles of Seth* (VII,5).

do with whether the *Gospel of Thomas* is largely dependent on the canonical gospels, in which case one might relax and seek to ignore it as purely secondary, or whether it is an independent source of information about the historical Jesus, in which case one should tighten one's belt, perhaps even learn Coptic, and bite the bullet.

Clearly the *Gospel of Thomas* does contain sayings that cannot be derived from the canonical gospels, since they are not there to be found. Yet, among these sayings are some that are clearly not Gnostic, but have the same claim to being old, even authentic, as does the older layer of sayings in the canonical gospels and Q. This can be illustrated by some of the kingdom parables in the *Gospel of Thomas*.[39] For example *Thom.* 97 reads: "The kingdom of the [Father] is like a woman who is carrying a [jar] filled with flour. While she was walking on [the] way, very distant (from home), the handle of the jar broke (and) the flour leaked out [on] the path. (But) she did not know (it); she had not noticed a problem. When she reached her house, she put the jar down on the floor (and) found it empty." In *Thom.* 98 we read: "The kingdom of the Father is like a person who wanted to kill a powerful person. He drew the sword in his house (and) stabbed it into the wall to test whether his hand would be strong (enough). Then he killed the powerful one." Such sayings are not Gnostic inventions, but simply part of the oral tradition of sayings ascribed to Jesus.

What is perhaps even more impressive is that the *Gospel of Thomas* contains some New Testament parables found in their pre-canonical form, that is to say, without Mark's secondary allegorical embellishments.[40] *Thom.* 9, the parable of the sower, lacks the allegorical interpretation appended in Mark 4:13–20. *Thom.* 65, the parable of the vineyard,

---

39. See C.-H. Hunzinger, "Unbekannte Gleichnisse Jesu aus dem Thomas-Evangelium," in *Judentum, Urchristentum, Kirche: Festschrift für Joachim Jeremias*, 2d. ed. Beihefte zur Zeitschrift für die neutestamentliche Wissenschaft 26, ed. W. Eltester (Berlin: Töpelmann, 1964), 209–20.

40. See C.-H. Hunzinger, "Außersynoptisches Traditionsgut im Thomas-Evangelium," *Theologische Literaturzeitung* 85 (1960): 843–46.

lacks the allegory of history with which the parable in Mark 12:1–11 is so permeated that even a rather conventional exegete, Werner Georg Kümmel, despaired of being able to disengage a nonallegorical core that could go back to Jesus.[41] But now the *Gospel of Thomas* presents us with just such a nonallegorical parable that may well go back to Jesus! Obviously the *Gospel of Thomas* was still in the flowing stream of oral tradition, and was not limited to canonical gospels, themselves often secondary, and to Gnostic mythology as its sources.[42]

The completely untenable position into which one can in all innocence flounder by ignoring the *Gospel of Thomas* is illustrated by an anecdote from the 1984 meeting of the Society for New Testament Studies in Basel, Switzerland. There, Nikolaus Walter of the University of Jena presented a detailed analysis of all instances of Paul using sayings of Jesus, irrespective of whether one is to consider them authentic or not. Having been asked to be the respondent, I pointed out that all the sayings of Jesus that Walter listed were derived from the canonical gospels, none of which had been written when Paul wrote. Obviously, Paul was wholly dependent on oral tradition or noncanonical written sources. Hence sayings ascribed to Jesus outside the canon should be included.

Walter asked for an instance. What I came up with on the spur of the moment was 1 Cor. 2:9: "But, as it is written, 'What no eye has seen, nor ear heard, nor the human heart conceived, what God has prepared for those who love him.'" The nearest one had come to identifying the source is Origen's allusion to an *Apocalypse of Elijah* (cited in the

---

41. W. G. Kümmel, "Das Gleichnis von den bösen Weingärtnern (Mark 12.1–5)," *Aux Sources de la tradition chrétienne: Mélanges offerts à M. Maurice Goguel à l'occasion de son soixante dixième anniversaire* (Neuchâtel: Delachaux et Niestlé, 1950), 120–31.

42. See Stephen J. Patterson, *The Gospel of Thomas and Jesus* (Sonoma, Calif.: Polebridge, 1993), especially chap. 2. "A Question of Content: The Autonomy of the Thomas Tradition," 17–93.

margin of the Nestle-Aland *Novum Testamentum Graece*).[43] But now it has cropped up as a saying of Jesus in *Thom.* 17: "I will give you what no eye has seen, and what no ear has heard, and what no hand has touched, and what has not occurred to the human mind." Should 1 Cor. 2:9 not be included in a survey of Pauline verses parallel to sayings ascribed to Jesus?

Walter replied that Paul does not quote 1 Cor. 2:9 as a saying of Jesus. I reminded him that a whole section of his paper had been devoted to Pauline parallels not ascribed by Paul to Jesus, such as 1 Cor. 13:2, about faith that moves mountains, but that are ascribed to Jesus in the canonical gospels, in this case Matt. 17:20; 21:21 // Mark 11:23. Should he not also include noncanonical instances?

Walter finally conceded the point. But when he published his revised paper, it was in this regard unaltered.[44] What could he do? After all, I had handed him a can of worms! Was he, in revising his paper for publication, to go through the whole *Gospel of Thomas,* not to speak of other non-canonical sources, looking for sayings ascribed to Jesus with Pauline parallels? It would be a rather hopeless undertaking! This is just one illustration of the challenges that the Nag Hammadi codices pose to anyone who wishes to forge a more complete picture of the discipline.

A decade later, at the 1995 meeting of the Society for

---

43. See *The Books of Elijah Parts 1–2,* comp. and trans. Michael E. Stone and John Strugnell, SBL Texts and Translations 18, Pseudepigrapha Series 8, ed. Robert A. Kraft and Harold W. Attridge (Missoula, Mont.: Scholars Press, 1979), 41–73 for the many attestations for this saying. In Nag Hammadi it recurs in I,1: A,23–27 (pp. 58–59) and III,5: 140,1–4 (pp. 56–57), in the latter case also ascribed to Jesus, as it is also in other texts (pp. 50–53). See also Takashi Onuki, "Traditionsgeschichte von Thomasevangelium 17 und ihre christologische Relevanz," in *Anfänge der Christologie: für Ferdinand Hahn zum 65. Geburtstag,* ed. Cilliers Breitenbach und Henning Paulsen (Göttingen: Vandenhoeck & Ruprecht, 1991), 399–415, and Patterson, *Gospel of Thomas and Jesus,* 85, and the extensive literature cited by both.

44. Nikolaus Walter, "Paulus und die urchristliche Jesustradition," *New Testament Studies* 31 (1975): 498–522.

New Testament Studies in Prague, Czech Republic, I convinced Barbara Aland, who was preparing a revised edition of Kurt Aland's *Synopsis Quattuor Evangeliorum,* not just to include a very good Greek retroversion of parallel sayings from the Coptic *Gospel of Thomas* that the Berliner Arbeitskreis, now under the responsibility of Hans-Gebhard Bethge, was preparing for her, but also to include (instead of the Latin translation, and alongside new German and English translations) the Berliner Arbeitskreis's critical edition of the Coptic text of the *Gospel of Thomas* itself. I had cited to her as a North American instance John S. Kloppenborg's *Q Parallels.*[45] She subsequently wrote on a very positive note:[46]

> The stimulating discussion with you has brought me now to think over basically once again the whole question of the revision of the *Synopse* and in this connection to study Kloppenborg. I am thoroughly impressed by the way he proceeds. To be sure, I would not like to offer a translation for all parallel passages, but it is advisable no doubt in Coptic.... The Aland *Synopsis* must be worked over in regard both to Nag Hammadi and to the Old Testament apocrypha.

As a result, the new edition of Aland's *Synopsis* appeared early in 1997, containing as the first of the appendices "Evangelium Thomae Copticum," presenting in a three-column format the Coptic original, alongside the German and English translations, and then, at the bottom of the page, the retroversion into Greek of sayings that have a parallel in the canonical gospels.[47] Hence not only North Americans have to stare the Coptic text of the *Gospel of Thomas* in

---

45. John S. Kloppenborg, *Q Parallels: Synopsis, Critical Notes and Concordance* (Sonoma, Calif.: Polebridge Press, 1988).

46. In a letter of 4 October 1995.

47. *Synopsis Quattuor Evangeliorum: Locis parallelis evangeliorum apocryphorum et patrum adhibitis,* ed. Kurt Aland, 15th rev. ed. (Stuttgart: Deutsche Bibelgesellschaft, 1996, 2d corrected printing, 1997), 517–46.

the face when we use Kloppenborg's *Q Parallels,* but world-wide New Testament scholarship has to face up to the Coptic text in using the standard tool for the scholarly study of the gospels as a whole, the *Synopsis* of Aland.

North American New Testament scholarship has come a long, long way, when the German establishment turns to an American publication as a role model! This coming of age of American biblical scholarship over the last half-century[48] is to a considerable extent due to the Nag Hammadi codices.[49]

---

48. After the SBL presentation R. McL. Wilson listed to me distin-guished American New Testament scholars of preceding generations, to relativize talk of the discipline only now coming of age in America. But the scope of the presentation was that of the sociology of knowledge, the structures of the discipline, not individuals, where one can only agree heartily with Wilson. Among our predecessors my own role model is, at least for me, preeminent: Ernest Cadman Colwell. Indeed, a major part of his distinction consisted in his involving himself actively in such a re-structuring of the discipline, in his specialization, New Testament textual criticism: he organized the International Greek New Testament Project and implemented it by means of the ongoing textual critical seminar of SBL. His coming to grips with the restructuring called for in terms of the soci-ology of knowledge would have been even more prominent if it had not taken place in the generation dominated by biblical theology on the right and demythologizing, existentialistic hermeneutics on the left.

49. Lüdemann, *Heretics,* 230 n. 9: "It was a truly historical moment when at the Annual Meeting of the Society of Biblical Literature in San Francisco in December 1977 this pioneering work of North American bib-lical scholarship was presented to the public. It made symbolically clear that the former predominance of German exegesis had come to an end forever."

For Further Reading

Kurt Aland, ed. *Synopsis Quattuor Evangeliorum.* 15th rev. ed. Stuttgart: Deutsche Bibelgesellschaft, 1996, 2d corrected printing, 1997. This is the standard synopsis of the four gospels used by scholars around the world. The newly revised edition contains for the first time an appendix (pp. 515–46) by the Berliner Arbeitskreis für koptisch-gnostische Schriften, including their critical Coptic text of *Thomas,* as well as their translation of the Coptic back into Greek (of the sayings with parallels in the New Testament), and their translations of all 114 sayings into German and English, from which the English translation presented in the present volume is derived. The appendix also contains the Greek fragments of *Thomas* found in Oxyrhynchus Papyri 1, 654, and 655.

Stevan Davies. *The Gospel of Thomas and Christian Wisdom.* New York: Seabury, 1983. A study of how *Thomas* makes use of ideas from Hellenistic Jewish wisdom theology, such as one finds, for example, in the Alexandrian Jewish theologian Philo.

Francis T. Fallon, and Ron Cameron. "The Gospel of Thomas: A Forschungsbericht and Analysis." In *Aufstieg und Niedergang der römischen Welt 2/25,* no. 6. Edited by W. Haase and W. Temporini. Berlin and New York: De Gruyter, 1988, pp. 4213–24. An excellent review of scholarship on the *Gospel of Thomas* in a number of different areas.

John S. Kloppenborg, Marvin W. Meyer, Stephen J. Patterson, and Michael G. Steinhauser. *Q-Thomas Reader.* Sonoma, Calif.: Polebridge, 1990. An introductory vol-

ume for persons interested in learning more about Q and
the Gospel of Thomas.

Helmut Koester. *Ancient Christian Gospels: Their History and Development.* Philadelphia: Trinity; London:
SCM, 1990. This volume represents the "state of the art"
in gospel research, covering the widest range of gospel
literature in early Christianity, including the Gospel of
Thomas.

Bentley Layton, ed. *Nag Hammadi Codex II,2–7 Together
with XII,2 Brit. Lib. Or. 4926 (1), and P. Oxy 1,
654, 655,* Vol. 1, *Gospel According to Thomas, Gospel
According to Philip, Hypostasis of the Archons, and In-
dexes.* Nag Hammadi Studies 20. Leiden: Brill, 1989.
This volume contains the standard critical edition of the
Coptic text of *Thomas* as well as the Greek fragments.
It also contains excellent introductions to the *Gospel of
Thomas* (by Helmut Koester) and the Greek fragments of
Thomas (by Harry Attridge).

Marvin Meyer. *The Gospel of Thomas: The Hidden Sayings of Jesus.* San Francisco: HarperSanFrancisco, 1992.
Meyer's text and translation of *Thomas* are highly re-
garded. Equally valuable in this edition are Meyer's
critical notes, which explain many obscurities in the text.

Stephen J. Patterson. *The Gospel of Thomas and Jesus.*
Sonoma, Calif.: Polebridge, 1993. Patterson locates the
Gospel of Thomas within the diverse developments of
early Christianity, and traces the *Thomas* trajectory from
the early social radicalism of the Jesus movement in
Palestine to the emergence of ascetic Christianity in Syria.

James M. Robinson and Marvin W. Meyer, eds., *The Nag
Hammadi Library in English,* trans. Coptic Gnostic Li-
brary Project of the Institute for Antiquity and Christian-
ity (Leiden: Brill, 1977 [pbk. ed. 1984]; San Francisco:
Harper & Row, 1977 [pbk. ed. 1981]); 3d rev. ed., ed.
James M. Robinson and Richard Smith (San Francisco:
Harper & Row; Leiden: Brill, 1988 [HarperCollins pbk.
ed. 1990]); reprinted unaltered as 4th rev. ed. (Leiden:
Brill, 1996). This volume is the standard translation of

the Nag Hammadi library into English. Included are an introduction to the entire collection (James M. Robinson) and brief introductions to each of the individual texts by leading scholars in the fields of Gnosticism and Nag Hammadi studies.

James M. Robinson, and Helmut Koester. *Trajectories through Early Christianity.* Philadelphia: Fortress, 1971. Robinson and Koester's pioneering essays redefining the shape and scope of the study of Christian origins. Many of these studies make creative use of the *Gospel of Thomas* in reshaping the discussion.

Richard Valantasis. *The Gospel of Thomas.* New Testament Readings. London and New York: Routledge, 1997. The most recent commentary on the Gospel of Thomas. Valantasis takes an approach consistent with the Routledge series in which this volume appears, which focuses more on reading strategies and less on traditional exegesis.

R. McL. Wilson. *Studies in the Gospel of Thomas.* London: A. R. Mowbray, 1960. An early look at the *Gospel of Thomas* by one of the world's eminent scholars of Gnosticism and early Christianity.

Index of Ancient Sources

Index of Authors

118